Rolls-Royce Spirituality

Rolls-Royce Spirituality

Transcending Mundane Faith

H. NEWTON MALONY

RESOURCE *Publications* • Eugene, Oregon

ROLLS-ROYCE SPIRITUALITY
Transcending Mundane Faith

Copyright © 2014 H. Newton Malony. All rights reserved. Except for brief quotations in critical publications or reviews, no part of this book may be reproduced in any manner without prior written permission from the publisher. Write: Permissions. Wipf and Stock Publishers, 199 W. 8th Ave., Suite 3, Eugene, OR 97401.

Resource Publications
An Imprint of Wipf and Stock Publishers
199 W. 8th Ave., Suite 3
Eugene, OR 97401

www.wipfandstock.com

ISBN 13: 978-1-62564-483-1

Manufactured in the U.S.A.

To the late Ivoloy Bishop

A Man of Faith; My Best-Man

"I came that they may have life, and have it abundantly." – Jesus Christ

(JOHN 3:13, NRSV)

"...this one thing I do: forgetting what lies behind and straining forward to what lies ahead, I press on toward the goal for the prize of the heavenly call of God in Christ Jesus." St. Paul

(PHILLIPIANS 3:13, NRSV)

Contents

Preface | ix
Introduction: My Dream Car; My Church Faith | xi

   1 SPIRITUALITY: A Christian Understanding | 1
   2 LOVE: The Umbrella Fruit | 10
   3 SELF-CONTROL: The Foundation Fruit | 20
   4 JOY: The Mood Fruit | 28
   5 PEACE: The Referee Fruit | 34
   6 PATIENCE: The Fisherman Fruit | 42
   7 KINDNESS: The Samaritan Fruit | 50
   8 GENEROSITY: The Stewardship Fruit | 57
   9 GENTLENESS: The Tenderizing Fruit | 64
10 FAITHFULNESS: The Practice Makes Perfect Fruit | 72

Bibliography | 81

Preface

I DEDICATED THIS VOLUME to the late Ivoloy Bishop and called him a Man of Faith and my Best-Man. Both are true.

Bishop was a Southern Baptist minister and, in the 1940s, was the Southwide Secretary of the Royal Ambassadors (the RAs)—that denomination's missionary organization for boys. I was a member of that organization and he functioned as a father-surrogate for me. My father had died when I was six years old. His friendship and care led me to affirm with gusto the RA Pledge of Allegiance:

I pledge myself to try to live worthily of the name of our order:

to guard my lips against profanity and untruth;

to keep my body clean and useful;

to study the lives of noble ambassadors set forth in God's Word and in world history;

to give what I can to support missions and by every possible deed to help bring in Christ's kingdom.

I assert my allegiance to Jesus Christ, my desire to live for Him and serve Him always.

I will "Live pure, Speak truth, Right wrong, for Christ the King

else wherefore born?

I make no claim to have always been faithful in the practice of this pledge, but I do know for sure that Ivoloy Bishop and the Royal Ambassadors had a significant influence on my decisions

Preface

to remain a life-long Christian, to become a Methodist minister and to ask Ivoloy to be my Best Man in my wedding of my wife of sixty years.

This volume on Rolls Royce Spirituality should be considered a workbook for serious Christians. It is meant to be use as a guide for daily Christian living as understood by Paul's list of Spiritual Fruit in Galatians 5. The book can be used for small-group or individual study of each chapter in the order they are listed in the Table of Contents. Another option would be to read the first four chapters, then select from the remaining chapters dealing specific spiritual fruit in the order one chooses.

To further explain this possibility: the first four chapters provide a basis for the rest of the book. These chapters are

Introduction—that considers the motive for my writing and the themes of the chapters that will follow;

Chapter 1: Spirituality: a Christian Expose—that discusses the unique way the Christian faith understands "the Spirit;"

Chapter 2: Love: the Umbrella fruit—that notes that Paul lists "Love" first in his list because it sums up the root meaning of all the other fruit;

Chapter 3: Self-Control: the Foundation fruit—that reflects on the way that self-control must always be in place for Love to be expressed.

After readers have considered each of these chapters they can then decide in which order they will consider the rest of Paul's list (Joy, Peace, Kindness, Gentleness, Generosity, Patience, and Faithfulness).

I hope readers will seriously think about joining me in trying to transcend mundane faith and mastering the way the Fruit of the Spirit can truly influence the way they live the Christian life. It can become a pilgrimage with much blessing.

H. Newton Malony, Trinity Season, 2014

Introduction
My Dream Car; My Church Faith

IN A SENSE, THIS is a book about me and my desire to transcend my mundane faith. I have been a part of the church almost all my life. My mother took me back to church the Sunday after my father's death when I was six years old and I have been there ever since. I know the church inside and out and have listened to literally thousands of sermons—both good and not-so-good. I have been a journeyman Christian. This is what I call "mundane faith."

But as time has gone by I have wondered what else might be in store for me if I really got serious about being the Christian Jesus called for in Matthew 5:48 when he stated, "Be perfect, therefore as your father in heaven is perfect.[1]" Similarly, as a Christian within the Wesleyan tradition, I have wondered what it might look like if I truly aspired to go beyond my present faith and become "sanctified." This was John Wesley's term for perfection—a state he challenged all Christians to try to reach five minutes before they died.

Strangely enough, as I lay in my bed thinking about these matters, my long time aspirations to own a perfect automobile came to mind. Don't ask me why, it just did. Like many American boys I grew up dreaming of the day when I would have a car to

1. Matt 5:48.

Introduction

drive. Early on, I owned a model A with a rumble seat followed by a 1934 Ford Coupe. But I always wanted something better. I even fantasized myself driving a Rolls-Royce some day. Don't laugh. In my mind, apart from its sleek lines, its massive grill, its wood-grain dash, its hand-sewn leather seats, and its ornate lights, it has always seemed to me to be automobile transportation as it was meant to be. And I, as a boy, fantasized that I was meant to be the driver. Alas, after a lifetime of cars, it has never happened. I have owned only one new car –a 1952 Nash Statesman—and the rest have been hand-me-downs of the Chevrolet/Plymouth variety. Yet, boyhood dreams never die, although they do, indeed, fade a little over time.

I was surprised how easily these fantasies about driving the ideal automobile came to mind as I thought of my interest in transcending my mundane faith and becoming an ideal Christian. If driving a Rolls-Royce car, such as the 1924 Silver Shadow pictured below, is what driving was meant to be, maybe aspiring toward sanctification is what the Christian faith as it, too was meant to be.

1907 Rolls-Royce Silver Ghost

I had to admit that the comparison was not as outlandish as it might seem.

Introduction

Because I am a spiritual man—Christian, to be exact. My faith is probably as important to me as the cars I drive. But, I do have to admit that heretofore I have spent no time or energy comparing the two. I have been content with a Pauline-type of faith that has emphasized the forgiveness of sins rather than the achievement of perfection. Frankly, I have been a Chevrolet Christian who existed with no aspirations toward a Rolls-Royce spirituality. I have been content to live by the adage "I love to sin, God loves to forgive; isn't it wonderful that the world is made that way?" Not that I have intentionally committed gross sins, such as John Newton—the former slave trader converted under John Wesley who wrote the hymn Amazing Grace. Oh, I have sung with fervor ". . . how sweet the sound that saved a wretch like me," but I didn't really think the label really applied to me.

Now don't get me wrong, Chevrolets are good cars and I have kept a pretty good shine on the outward appearances of my faith. In fact, I am known as a very good, if not excellent, churchman. My name and picture is in the church directory. You will find me in church most Sundays. I give money; I serve on committees. I even give religious talks every now and then. Recently, I even served as an adult mentor in the Confirmation Class. I am a good journeyman Christian. I look with disdain at cars that pass by my church on the way to the beach or mountains on Sunday mornings. My Chevrolet religion is not all that bad, thank you.

But I would pause if someone asked me why I didn't aspire to as high a standard for my religion as I do for the automobiles I drive. I dream of driving a Rolls-Royce but am content with a Chevrolet faith. I know the teachings that we are "saved by grace, through faith, and not by works lest anyone should boast."[2] Yet, I have used this teaching of Paul in Ephesians 2:8 to avoid ever being accused of "works righteousness." Certainly, I would never be one of those "professors" in Wesley's day that claimed they had achieved perfection. He wrote a tract cautioning these "professors" against such assertions.

2. Ephesians 2:8.

Introduction

But the question still haunted me. "Should I not desire for as much excellence in faith as I do in cars?" I have to admit I probably should. I feel a bit ashamed that I have never given much thought to this inconsistency. At the very least I ought to have asked "What would Rolls-Royce Spirituality look like?" "How would a transcended mundane faith change me?" "If I truly aspired to as high a standard in my religious life as I did in my automobiles would other people notice my achievement?" "What would I be doing that is different?" "How would I be feeling?" "In what new way would I be living?" These were the questions I asked myself as I considered deepening my faith.

BACK TO THE BIBLE FOR ANSWERS

I decided to give it a try. I felt led back to the Bible to see if there were some Rolls-Royce ideas about spiritual living that could be found there. I didn't have to look far. I discovered that my Chevrolet religion had been based on only half of what Paul had to say. In his first letter to the Corinthians (12:1 ff) Paul writes about Spiritual gifts. I eagerly searched his list in hopes I could transcend my mundane faith by aspiring to receive one or more of these gifts. Paul mentions "miracles," "uttering wisdom," "healing," "prophecy," and "speaking in, as well as interpreting, tongues," among others. I had to admit these were Rolls-Royce ideas, but they sure were scary. I wouldn't know where to begin. My mundane type of spirituality had never included knowing anybody who had any of these gifts. Paul seems to imply these could, and should, only be seen in church worship. He was very clear about when, where, and how these gifts were to be expressed. I had heard about this "charismatic" type of worship but had never experienced it.[3]

I read on in 1 Corinthians and was amazed to realize that Chapter 13 followed Paul's list of spiritual gifts. This was the very familiar "love chapter." Next to the Beatitudes, these beautiful words were probably among the best known verses in the Bible. This 13th

---

3. This is a bit of an exaggeration. I had a close friend in seminary and I once knew an Anglican pastor both of who spoke in tongues. .

chapter of 1 Corinthians was read at my wedding. However, when you realize that these words follow Paul's cautions about expressing spiritual gifts, you have to admit he intended these words to serve an entirely different purpose than blessing marital bliss. He was suggesting that these gifts were not to be paraded before others in any pompous manner but should be embedded within the motivation to "love."

I had often heard about love as God's will. I remembered the words of Jesus to the Pharisees that the first and greatest commandment was to ". . . love the Lord your God with all your heart, and with all your soul and with all your mind.[4]" Then I recalled that Jesus added the kicker that ". . . you shall love your neighbor as yourself.[5]" Whoa! I suddenly realized that this love of God and neighbor might be at the center of my effort to transcend mundane faith. This really scared me. I realized that these words I had repeated so often and so glibly in my religious practice might have to become realities if I really got serious about becoming a Rolls-Royce Christian. *Love* indeed! I had to sit down and reflect on what "love" might require of me.

Some of my recollections came to mind. Somewhere I had heard a humorous prayer of a little girl. She prayed: *"Dear God, I bet it is very hard for you to love everybody in the whole world. There are only four people in our family and I can never do it."*

Another was an incident Rachel Remen told in her book *My Grandfather's Blessing*. She became a good friend with Kenny, the young son of some friends. They played with two Hot Wheels cars that he adored. When these little cars started being given away with fill-ups by a nearby service station, Rachel had her friends obtain a number of Hot Wheels that she gave to Kenny on his birthday. He was delighted and put the cars all around the room. When she visited with Kenny several weeks later, she noted that he no longer played with these Hot Wheels cars. She asked him why.

---

4. Matt 22:34.
5. Matt 22:39.

Introduction

In a quivery voice he replied, "I don't know how to love this many cars, Rachel."[6]

These humorous anecdotes pale in importance to Jesus' parable of the Good Samaritan that he told to illustrate what love of the neighbor really was—caring for those who are strangers, even enemies. I decided that if love was essential to Rolls-Royce spirituality, it was going to be no simple matter. It was going to take sloughing through some pretty murky territory for me.

At the very least, it was going to take some serious reflection for me regarding the differences among liking and loving. I would have to get a better hold on "What transcending my mundane faith might demand of me?" as I tried to understand the love I had for my family, the appreciation I had for friends with whom I hiked mountains, the disdain I felt toward child sexual abusers and all other mixtures of feelings I had for the rest of those who crossed my path day by day.

ST. PAUL'S LIST OF THE FRUIT OF THE SPIRIT

But I was in my right mind when I set out on this journey and I decided I would be too embarrassed to turn around. Instead of giving up, I decided to search the Scriptures some more for further guidance about this love that Paul said had to underlie the gifts of the Holy Spirit. My search paid off in spades. I discovered that just as he had tied love with *gifts* of the Holy Spirit 1st Corinthians 13, so had he made love dominant in his list of the *fruit* of the Holy Spirit in his letter to the Galatians 5. What a find!

Here is what I read: *"By contrast, the fruit of the Spirit is love, joy, peace, patience, kindness, generosity, faithfulness, gentleness, and self-control. There is no law against such things."*[7]

At first I thought that *gifts* and *fruits* might be the same thing. A closer reading changed my mind. I read these strange words in Galatians 5:23 "There is no law against such things." This was

---

6. Remen, *My Grandfather's Blessing*, page #.
7. Galatians 5:22–24.

puzzling. This felt like an out-of-the-blue statement. I went back to Galatians 5 and read the words leading up to Paul's list of fruit. Then, the meaning of the statement about there being no law against the fruit of the Spirit made sense to me. Verses 19 ff read: *"Now the works of the flesh are obvious: fornication, impurity, licentiousness, idolatry, sorcery, enmities, strife, jealousy, anger, quarrels, dissensions, factions, envy, drunkenness, carousing, and things like these."*[8]

There was definitely a "law" against doing "such things" as these. Paul calls them "works of the flesh" or "doing what you want.[9]" My first thought about my mundane faith was that I was pretty safe from most of these. I was not a drunk; I didn't arouse; I didn't practice sorcery; I didn't fornicate; I didn't worship idols; I didn't have any enemies that I knew of; I wasn't very jealous; I didn't carouse; I was not envious; I didn't quarrel too much. I didn't know what licentiousness, factions, or dissension meant—but I was pretty sure I didn't do much of any of them. But not doing all of "these things" (as Paul called them) didn't feel like they would add up to Rolls-Royce Spirituality. As Paul stated in Galatians 5:16ff, *"Live by the Spirit, I say, and do not gratify the desires of the flesh. For what the flesh desires is opposed to the Spirit, and what the Spirit desires is opposed to the flesh."*[10]

It dawned on me: true Spirituality requires more than a set of behaviors one does *not* do. Spirituality is a set of behaviors that one *does*. This is where Paul's list of *fruit* comes into play. They are a set of behaviors one should do if they are ever to achieve Rolls-Royce Spirituality.

And probably most important, these fruit are to be expressed anywhere, anytime; everywhere, every time. Wow! No holds barred! That truth is both freeing and challenging. I am free from worrying about whether I violate any of the prohibitions and challenged to be vigilant about trying to express all the fruit in every contact I have in my daily life.

8. Galatians 5:19.
9. Galatians 5:18.
10. Galatians 5:16.

Introduction

PRACTICING THE FRUIT OF THE SPIRIT

What a list! I decided he left nothing out of the panorama of feelings and actions I engaged in throughout any given day. My first thought was, "I could give Paul's list a try." I already do some of these things. I'm a pretty loving, joyful, peaceful, patient, kind, generous, faithful, gentle, self-controlled guy. I could rev-up my practice of them a bit. I could do it. I'm a pretty good, everyday Christian. No one could ever accuse me of not being willing to try. Becoming a Rolls-Royce Christian might not be so hard after all.

Continuing my initial reaction to Paul's list, I became aware that not one of them referred to what I did on Sunday as I became active in being a regular, mundane Christian. There was no mention of church attendance, going on a mission trip, visiting the sick, studying the Bible, voting for peace and justice, attending prayer meeting, or teaching Sunday School. This was OK with me. I was getting a bit weary of some of those things, anyway. To know that Paul didn't think they were too important was somewhat of a relief.

So, I set about reading and re-reading Paul's statement about the *fruit of the Holy Spirit* hoping against hope that the way out of mundane faith was straight-forward and easy. Boy, was I wrong. It turned out that Paul began with that old bug-a-boo word *Love* and it got more problematic as I read through the list. Paul knew how difficult achieving such well known ideals as "patience," "generosity," and "kindness," (not to mention "love" and "self-control") could be. I discovered that the effort to achieve Rolls-Royce spirituality was going to be a struggle, to say the least.

FRUIT OF THE SPIRIT AS A GUIDE TO ROLLS-ROYCE SPIRITUALITY

I began the enterprise by considering each of Paul's Spiritual fruit one at a time. I decided each fruit should become a separate set of reflections and prescriptions. I gave each fruit a label that explained it initially. My beginning list looked like this:

Love –the *Umbrella* fruit

Introduction

    Joy—the *Mood* fruit
    Peace—the *Referee* fruit
    Patience—the *Fisherman* fruit
    Kindness—the *Samaritan* fruit
    Generosity—the S*tewardship* fruit
    Faithfulness—the *Practice makes perfect* fruit
    Gentleness—the *Tenderizing* fruit
    Self-control—the *Foundation* fruit.

However, as I thought about this list, it occurred to me that the first (Love) and the last (Self-control) were basic to all the rest. In fact, these two were like the accelerator and the brake on my idolized Rolls-Royce car. The accelerator (Love) propelled the car forward; i.e., gave it the gas to move down the road while the brake (Self-control) stopped the car to keep an accident from occurring. The other Spiritual fruit were like the various components of the motor that must coordinate with one another to carry the car from place to place.

With *Love* and *Self-control* in mind, I decided I would reflect on these in the beginning, and then consider each of the other fruits. Another way of saying it would be: *Joy, Peace, Patience, Kindness, Generosity, and Gentleness* tell us what *Love* would look like provided persons had *themselves* under *Control*. I decided the last chapter should be *Faithfulness*. Last is where Paul put it. I called it the *Practice Makes Perfect* fruit. Continuing to use the Rolls-Royce analogy, this final chapter on *Faithfulness* will consider the truth that skilled driving always depends on being faithful in getting out on the road and *Practicing*. Likewise, truly transcending mundane faith through Rolls-Royce *Spirituality* will be based on faithful practice of the spiritual fruits in daily life.

One further preliminary thought came to mind as I anticipated my venture into these components of Rolls-Royce Spirituality. I wondered if I was as clear as I ought to be on the root meaning of the word "Spirituality." After all, Galatians 5 says these are the "fruit of *The Spirit*."[11] I asked myself "What is the *Spirit in Spirituality?*" Is S*pirit* some kind of basic 'stuff' that produces "fruit" in a

11. Galatians 5.

Introduction

similar way that rich potting soil stimulates the growth of gardens. That feels funny but it sounded right. *Spirit* is the context surrounding, provoking, under-girding, penetrating, and causing the *fruit* to ripen. Moreover, *Spirit* is the root that explains the fruit; the context that explains the content. I decided I needed to become clearer about the nature of the *Spirit* in Rolls-Royce SPIRITUALITY before I dealt with how it produced Love, Joy, Peace, Patience, Kindness, Generosity, Faithfulness, Gentleness and Self-Control. Thus, before the chapters on Love and Self Control I will include a chapter on Spirituality. I have labeled this *a Christian Understanding* in order to distinguish it from spirituality of any other kind.

Think of this chapter on "Spirituality," therefore, not as a digression but as a necessary foundation for the plan to reflect more specifically about Rolls-Royce Spirituality as conceived by Saint Paul in the fruit of the Spirit in Galatians 5.

I hope you, the reader, will find the following as invigorating and inspiring.

1

SPIRITUALITY
A Christian Understanding

I DON'T KNOW HOW many times I have heard people say, "I believe in being a *spiritual* person but I am not *religious.*" These folk seem to me to be using the term *spiritual* in a way that doesn't make sense to me. I want to be *spiritual* and *religious*. After all, I am a Christian and Galatians 5 is a letter written to Christians. I want my "spirituality" to make sense to me "religiously" in other words, to my Christian religious faith. That is who I want to be when I aspire to Rolls-Royce *Spirituality.*

A MODEL FOR WHAT IT MEANS TO HAVE A "SPIRITUAL" EXPERIENCE

I once heard a professor talk about religious experience that may help in understanding being a spiritual, as well as a religious, person. Let's see if it might assist us in this discussion. He said that all human beings experience "empirical reality" every day. Empirical reality is the kind of experience that comes to us through the five senses of taste, sight, hearing, touch, and smell. Through the miracle of our minds we turn these sensations into perceptions that, thus, make sense of the world in which we live from day to day. So far, so good.

The professor said that in addition to our empirical experience, human beings have the capacity to experience trans-empirical reality. *Trans*-empirical is a type of experience that is above and beyond, or in addition to, the kind of reality that is based on the five senses. To be sure, it might be triggered by a sensation (such as sight or sound) but it goes beyond it. Some have called this type of experience 'supernatural.'

We all have these types of experiences when we dream. But usually trans-empirical, supernatural experiences come when we are wide awake. They resemble, yet go beyond, the world of imagination. Some people have reported these experiences as a sense of being one with nature when they viewed a beautiful sunset from a mountain top. Others have recounted feelings of sublime joy when their family gathered for a holiday meal or the inner peace they felt in quiet contemplation or eastern meditation. It is this type of experience that people often use in claiming to be "spiritual but not religious." These experiences are *Trans*- empirical, meaning they are different from the everyday 'empirical" reality. Another way of labeling these experiences is call them "altered states of consciousness."

The professor said that everyone had the capacity to have these types of experiences. I asked the professor whether he meant by using the word "capacity." "Why didn't you leave out that word "capacity" and just say, 'Everyone has these types of experiences?'" He replied, "I used the word "capacity" intentionally because I do not believe everyone has spiritual or trans-empirical experiences. Some people do, some people don't, but everyone has the capacity." He explained that capacity was another word for possibility or ability. These types of experience are possible, but not automatically probable. They are not necessary, essential, obligatory requirements for survival.

If what the professor said is true, you can live without spiritual experiences, and many people do. Thus, being spiritual is not a drive that must be satisfied, such as hunger. Much less is it an instinct, or else everyone would be spiritual in exactly the same way. Spiritual experience is a *capacity*—an ability or a possibility. But, it is not a necessity for daily life."

This was a surprise to me because these kinds of spiritual (trans-empirical) experiences were familiar to me and they had often occurred for me in overtly religious settings. I have had spiritual (trans-empirical) experiences:

- When I felt a call to full-time Christian service at a summer camp;
- When I heard Martin Luther King give his "I Have a Dream" speech at Riverside Church in New York City;
- When I pronounced a biblical blessing at my mother's side as she breathed her last breath;
- When a baby is baptized at a church service and the congregation pledges love and support;
- When I enter a beautiful sanctuary where symbols of the Alpha & Omega are displayed beneath a Xi and a Rho:
- When I hear an inspiring sermon.

MAKING SPIRITUAL EXPERIENCE "RELIGIOUS"

The professor cautioned me, however, against making any presumption that all spiritual experiences were religious. They are not, he said. In fact, he continued, "Trans-empirical, or spiritual experiences, can be once-in-a-lifetime emotional events for some people or transitory feelings that stand alone without any connection to church or religion." When he said this, I remembered reading about the reports of people engaging in TM (transcendental meditation) where folk simply reported feeling relaxed and enjoyed the euphoria of the experience, nothing more. I also recalled the Harvard study of the effects of psychedelic drugs where some had the fantasy they were helping Jesus shoulder His cross while other people just simply experienced out-of-body reverie.

What joins spiritual experiences with religion, my professor contended, is applying perceptions, concepts and rituals to the spiritual experience that give the event greater understanding and meaning as well as assure that the experience will occur over and over again. In fact, he suggested that this is a definition of "religion." A religion is the application of the words, concepts, rituals, and behaviors that help provide understanding and meaning to spiritual experiences. This definition would apply to all new as well as old religions:

- Hinduism as well as The Church Universal and Triumphant;
- Christianity as well as The Holy Spirit Association;
- Islam as well as Scientology;
- Judaism as well as Sikhism.

An intriguing biblical example is the story of Samuel answering the call of God in 1 Samuel 3:1ff. I am going to quote this episode below. I will use Eugene Peterson's *The Message* because it recounts the Bible in such understandable language:

> *The boy Samuel was serving God under Eli's (the priest) direction. This was a time when the revelation of God was rarely heard or seen. One night Eli was sound asleep (his eyesight was very bad—he could hardly see). It was well before dawn; the sanctuary lamp was still burning. Samuel was still in bed in the Temple of God, where the Chest of God rested.*
>
> *Then God called out, "Samuel, Samuel!"*
>
> *Samuel answered, "Yes, I'm here." Then he ran to Eli saying, "I heard you call. Here I am."*
>
> *Eli said, "I didn't call you, Go back to bed." And so he did.*
>
> *God called again, "Samuel, Samuel!"*
>
> *Samuel got up and went to Eli, "I heard you call. Here I am."*
>
> *Again Eli said, "Son, I didn't call you. Go back to bed." (This all happened before Samuel knew God for himself.*

> *It was before the revelation of God had been given to him personally).*
>
> *God called again, "Samuel!"—the third time. Yet again Samuel got up and went to Eli, "Yes, I heard you call me. Here I am."*
>
> *That's when it dawned on Eli that God was calling the boy. So Eli directed Samuel, "Go back and lie down. If the voice calls again, say, 'Speak, God. I'm your servant, ready to listen.'" Samuel returned to his bed.*
>
> *Then God came and stood before him exactly as before, calling out, "Samuel, Samuel!"*
>
> *Samuel answered, "Speak. I'm your servant, ready to listen."*[1]

This is a clear illustration of how a spiritual experience can be coupled with religious faith through the application of perceptions, concepts, words, and rituals to the event. The story contains subtle caveats that show the author knew that spiritual experience is simply another strange or awesome experience until meaning and understanding was applied to it. Note the phrase illustrating this truth: *"This all happened BEFORE Samuel knew God for himself"* (i.e., before Samuel had words that helped him understand the spiritual experience of hearing a voice in the night).

Also note what Eli did: *"If the voice calls again, say, Speak, God, I'm your servant, ready to listen"* (i.e., he gave Samuel words that framed the spiritual experience within a meaningful, religious context). When Eli told Samuel to say "Speak, Lord. . ." when he heard his name called in the middle of the night, he knew Samuel would know that "Lord" would not be a strange word to Samuel. He knew Samuel would know immediately that the "Lord" who would speak to him was the God of the Jewish faith—the God of Abraham, Issac, Jacob, Moses, Joshua. It was not some strange or unfamiliar deity speaking to him in the darkness of midnight. Spiritual experience and religion were joined.

When Samuel said *"Speak"* to the voice that called his name, he knew full-well the God who now spoke these fascinating words *"I am about to do something in Israel that will make both ears of*

---

1. Eugene Peterson, *The Message*, 398.

anyone who hears of it tingle.[2]" He believed in the words of the Jewish religion that told him about the God of Abraham, Issac, and Jacob. Samuel had never had direct experience with this God until told by Eli whose voice was calling his name. It was Jehovah. His spiritual experience was now a religious experience. By applying the words of his religious faith he understood his spiritual experience.

THE "SPIRITUAL" IN CHRISTIAN FAITH

We can use Samuel's experience to better understand St. Paul's use of the term "Spirit" in his list of "the fruit of the Spirit" in Galatians. Paul, like Eli in the Samuel story, probably assumed his readers would automatically know who the Spirit was in Spiritual fruit. After all, he was a Christian writing to Christians. And we today are Christians reading a Christian letter. Paul knew without asking that, when he used the word "Spiritual," he was referring to the Spirit of Jesus Christ, the Son of God. He knew he did not need to explain that "Spiritual" did not refer to some trans-empirical euphoria or altered state of consciousness resulting from watching a sunset or sitting cross-legged repeating "Om" over and over. It was the "Holy Spirit" of Almighty God, the Father of our Lord Jesus Christ. Paul assumed we would automatically know that the Spirit who would bear fruit in our lives was the *Spirit of the God who created us and whose will was embodied in Jesus Christ, our Lord and our Savior.* The work of this *Spirit* in our lives—this tying together of our Christian faith with our spiritual experience—is what can make it possible for us to transcend mundane Christian faith and actualize Rolls-Royce Spirituality.

THE TRINITY IN CHRISTIAN FAITH

Our Christian tradition has affirmed that the "Holy Spirit" is part of the Trinity; i.e., our God is God the Father, plus God the Son,

---

2. 1 Samuel 3:11.

plus God the Holy Spirit—three in one: one in three: the same but different; indivisible yet present in three ways.

Likely we have all seen this triangle representing the three dimensions of Father, Son, and Holy Spirit as three points with lines that distinguish them from one another yet which each relate to God at the center. In the above illustration the words are in Latin. Thus, Father (Pater), Son (Filius), Holy Spirit (Spiritus Sanctus—abbreviated), God (Deus) Is (Est) and Is Not (non est). It reads, in English, God is Father, God is Son, God is Holy Spirit. God is all three in One. But, the Father is not the Son or the Holy Spirit; the Son is not the Holy Spirit or The Father; the Holy Spirit is not the Father or the Son. To state each part of God's functioning is to say that God is creator, God is redeemer, and God is daily presence—different roles, nevertheless, all are God; three in One.

Therefore, the "Holy Spirit" in "Fruit of the Spirit"[3] is not some new divinity nor novel comforter—No! Here, Paul assumes we would know that Galatians "Spirit," both the God who was present in Creation (Father) and the God who was present in Redemption (the Son) reside in the background in their fullness as the God who works within us to produce spiritual "fruit."

To elaborate, Paul, like Eli, would know immediately that the "Spirit" Paul was talking about was of . . .

3. Gal 5:22ff.

Rolls-Royce Spirituality

>Almighty God whose intention for us was the same as it had always been since the dawn of creation when S/He "...*created humankind in his image...male and female he created them,*[4]" as well as of
>
>Almighty God whose redemption of us through Jesus had been realized when He "...*was in Christ, reconciling the world unto Himself.*[5]"

Thus, the "fruit(s)" that the Spirit produces are each a part of what God intended the human beings should be/do in creating them in the first place and who and what God intended in redeeming them through Jesus. This is the profound truth of Christian faith. All Christians know the head-waters of the stream that flows through them and are prepared to receive the living presence of the Almighty/Redeeming God in their daily lives through the Holy Spirit. This is the Holy Spirit—what moves in us through trans-empirical experience to produce fruit that ties us all the way back to the moment of our creation and redemption.

The unique role of this Holy Spirit of Almighty God is to enlighten, inspire, encourage, under gird, strengthen, redeem and restore us in our efforts to transcend mundane Christian faith and aspire toward Rolls-Royce "Spirituality." The "fruit" of *Love, Joy, Peace, Patience, Kindness, Generosity, Faithfulness, Gentleness, and Self-control* are but dimensions of practical steps that are incorporated, imbued, and empowered by the presence of the Holy Spirit. When we enter into this altered state of consciousness, this trans-empirical experience, we have the understandings that tie spirituality to religion and know the foundation of feelings we are experiencing.

Experiencing the Holy Spirit is what we do when we pray. We shut our eyes and enter into an altered state of consciousness and welcome the Holy Spirit into our consciousness. This trans-empirical experience results from our exercising our capacity to have an experience that goes beyond daily interactions based on sight, sound, taste, hearing, or touch. It can influence what we do

---

4. Gen 1:27.
5. 2 Cor 5:19.

when we open our eyes and return to daily life. Christians through the ages have known the absolute reality of these moments. They known that they have been in touch with the God who created them for a purpose; who continues to redeem and call them back from the tendency to selfish pursuits, and who penetrates their very existence to empower them moment by moment to do good. In other words, they have been in the presence of the Trinity (Father, Son, *and* Holy Spirit)

    We turn next our consideration of the several "fruit of the Holy Spirit." We begin with *Love, the Umbrella Fruit.*

2

LOVE
The Umbrella Fruit

I SHOULD FOREWARN YOU of the approach I will use in reflecting on the various fruit mentioned in Galatians 5. Perhaps, fore-*inform* would be a better word. The words used by St. Paul for each of the fruit are familiar to us and I would like to probe the day-to-day, practical meaning they might have for us. Whatever else God may be doing or have in mind for his kingdom on earth, I feel convinced that St. Paul was absolutely on-target in suggesting that we should aspire to show-forth the fruit he mentions in our daily interactions with other people who might cross our paths every day. I see these "fruit" as being aspects of our interactions with others with whom we rub shoulders. I leave to others to write about Rolls-Royce Spirituality as it applies to larger groups such as cities, states, nations, politics, social ethics, etc. These are significant arena for Rolls-Royce Spirituality but I will leave their implications to others. I intend to focus on day-to-day interpersonal interactions. In this approach, I see myself as following Paul's suggestion in Romans 12:1 (The Message)

LOVE

"*So here's what I want you to do, God helping you: Take your everyday, ordinary life—your sleeping, eating, . . . sleeping, eating, going to work, and walking around life—and place it before God as an offering.*[6]"

Let's begin with *Love*. I call Love the *umbrella fruit*. By this I mean to suggest that love covers all the other fruits like an Umbrella. In fact, it could be said that all the other fruits are actually implications of the ways love is practically expressed in human behavior. So, we begin with *Love,* knowing that its essence can be seen in all the other fruit. And, as a corollary, I will then deal with *Self-control*, the last fruit in Paul's list, as the *Foundation fruit* that can make-or-break the expression of love through *Joy, Peace, Patience, Kindness, Generosity, Faithfulness,* and *Gentleness*.

Love is a very common word. "Love" is used by us in a great variety of ways. "I *love* chocolate." "I *love* jazz music." "I have fallen in *love* a time or two." "I *love* to read detective stories." "I *love* chemistry." "I *love* to play in the snow." "I *love* my wife." "I *love* to play chess." "I *love* steak." "I *love* to travel." "I *love* my grandfather,"etc.

However, when we use *Love* in seeking to understand Rolls-Royce Spirituality we are talking about *loving other people*. Only three of the examples given above apply to other people: falling in love, loving my wife, loving my grandfather. Would these examples be significantly different from loving chocolate, chess, steak, traveling, or chemistry? You bet they would! Sweethearts, wives, and grandfathers are living, breathing, walking, talking human beings—just like us. Loving other people is a completely different experience from loving food, games, school subjects, sweets, etc. Loving other people is what the Bible meant when St. Paul described it in 1 Corinthians 13 and make it the first fruit in the Galatians 5 list toward which we are aspiring in our quest to become Rolls-Royce Spiritualists.

---

6. Rom 12:1–2 (The Message).

HOW LOVE DEVELOPS

It is this 'love of other people' that I intend for us to explore together. As I thought about this, I decided it might be fun to begin where we all begin—contact with one another—that time in human experience when the word is used for the first time. The famous psychologist, William James, said the obvious when he declared that in the beginning infants experience the world as a booming confusing conglomerate of meaningless sights and sounds. The first distinction infants make after only a short time of life outside the womb is the difference between pain and pleasure. We sense they are making this distinction when they become irritable and cry but calm down after being fed or having their diapers changed. We would be concerned if this did not happen. To say that infants "know" what they are doing would be premature. Making this distinction between pleasure and pain is very primitive, even instinctive. It is the foundation from which all sorts of other feelings emerge over a life time.

Probably, the first times infants hear the word *love* is from the mouth of a mother who is cuddling or feeding them. And it is mothers who say the word "love" to express *their* feelings toward their babies long before these mothers hear the word "love" said back to them. At that moment when infants do look their mothers in the eye and say *I love you*, the expression will be intricately related to the pleasure they have received from being fed or cuddled.

I am reminded of the very first poem I ever wrote. It was written some years after I had learned to speak and write—probably in the first or second grade. It goes like this:

I love my mother, she is so sweet. When I am hungry, she gives me a treat.

When I am sad, she makes me glad. I love my mother, she is so sweet.

This poem clearly states how my love of my mother was related to her meeting my basic needs. I have no doubt that what was true for me would be true for most other people. The love that children have for their parents is grounded in the care, support, guidance, provision, etc. they have been given by their parents through the years. In a sense, this love is but a more sophisticated expression of infants' recognition of who brought them pleasure when they were in pain. Most often, when children become adults and express *love* to their own infants, they do so out of the memory of their parents' love of them.

LOVE DIFFERS FROM "LIKE"

What this analysis does not make clear is whether, or how, "love" is different from "like." For example, most children would say "I love my father" but "I like my soccer coach." They know and feel the difference even though they might not be able to fully describe it. Probably, they could say what they "liked" about their coach but would be less specific about why they "loved" their father. I would guess they would quickly say, "He's my father," as if their love for him was self-explanatory.

It would seem important, in aspiring toward Rolls-Royce Spirituality, to fully understand how love and like are different since "love" heads the list of St. Paul's Spiritual fruit and nowhere does he mention "like." Nowhere does Paul allude to "like" as a goal to which we should aspire. I doubt the Good Samaritan[7] "liked" the Jew who fell among thieves. But his stopping to bind up the traveler's wounds and take him to a Jericho inn were used to illustrate the Samaritan's "love" of his neighbor—even a neighbor he had never seen. Furthermore, there is the curious situation recently reported in the news where a mother confessed to Dear Abbey that she loved, but did not like, her daughter. It seems her daughter reminded her of her former husband who left her during the pregnancy.

I would like to propose that both the Good Samaritan and this mother got it right—"loving" has little to do with "liking." Is it not true that when we say we "like" somebody we are talking about something about them that pleases us? It could be something they

---

7. Cf Luke 10:30ff.

have done for us or some opinion they have with which we agree. It could be a reaction to something they have done or their style in doing a particular task. It could be their help in some task we undertake together or some way they dress. When people let us in line in traffic, give us good service in a restaurant, send us a birthday present, deliver an interesting lecture, help us load our groceries in the car, and in a myriad of other ways please us, we say we "like" them. And when we give it some thought we know that this "liking" of others dates back to our infancy when we first made the distinction between pleasure and pain.

LOVE IS A PRE-EXISTING ATTITUDE BASED IN IDENTITY

But 'love' is something different. Most parents will state that they loved their children even before they were born. Certainly, they did not wait to love their babies until they walked, talked, danced, earned good grades, excelled in sports, or played instruments in recitals—all those things that children do to please their parents. Most parents love their children all along the way from changing diapers to attending graduation exercises. 'Love' is a pre-existing attitude or feeling that mothers and fathers bring with them as they relate to their children. 'Love' is what the Good Samaritan brought with himself as he traveled the road from Jerusalem to Jericho. 'Love' is that set of feelings and attitudes Paul recommended Christians put at the top of the list in their efforts to be truly spiritual.

Knowing, however, that 'love' implies we are to have loving feelings and loving attitudes toward others *before* they do anything that pleases us (i.e., brings us pleasure) still leaves the content of 'love' unexplained. I would like to propose that 'love' is based on *identity* as contrasted with 'liking' that is based on *pleasure*. Let me see if you agree.

When I state that *identity* is the basis of love I believe the love we are to have for our neighbors stems from the 'identity' love we received from our parents who created us. We are flesh of our

LOVE

parents' flesh. We exist as their offspring and look like them. This is our *identity*. They love what they have created. The same is true, more fundamentally, of God's love for us. He created us in His image. We look like Him. We exist only because He acted. We are His children. This is our *identity*. God loves what God has created.[8]

IDENTITY LOVE ELABORATED

The love we are called to share with others stems from the *identity love* we received from our parents who begat us and from God who created us in His image. We are called to love those in our family because of their flesh and blood identity as our brothers and sisters. We *identify* with them because of their *identity*. We are called to love our neighbors because we share the divine image with them—we share their identity as God's creations. I state again: We *identify* with them because of their *identity*[9] This *identity love* is that set of pre-existing attitudes and feelings that we are called to bring to all our relationships with other human beings—both inside the family and outside in the world. This *identity love* is what the Good Samaritan had with him on the Jericho Road. This *identity love* is what Paul would have us embody as the prime essence of attaining Rolls-Royce Spirituality. All the other fruit of the Holy Spirit are but practical ingredients of this fundamental type of love.

---

8. God's love of us is based on the act of Creation where God said, "Let us make humankind in our image, according to our likeness. . .So God created humankind in his image, in the image of God he created them, male and female he created them" (Genesis 1:26a-27, NRSV). Whenever we say "We are God's children" this is what we mean. God created the whole earth; everything that is. But one thing, and only one thing, did God create "in His image," i.e., human beings. God is truly, absolutely, realistically our Father. He loves us as a parent.

9. This idea bears a Christian similarity to the Sikh word "Namaste." Sikhs state this word as a greeting when they meet other people. It stands for an awareness that they recognize the divine spark that resides in every person.

IDENTITY LOVE PRECEDES LIKING

Now, does it need to be said that this *identity love* precedes and is apart from any *pleasure liking* we may have for those with whom we come into contact? I hope not, but growing to say we love on the basis of what pleases us is very seductive. Do we like them or not? Do we admit we acknowledge them or not? Do they matter to us or not? We have many adjectives to describe other people: young, old, handsome, beautiful, smart, dumb, nice, dirty, helpful, hateful, ugly, well-dressed, black, white, good, bad, etc., etc. These adjectives often guide our reactions to others. *Identity Love* calls for us to do away with all our adjectives. We love them because of who they are—our brothers, our sisters, created by God to show forth His image in our daily life. This is the feeling we who would be Rolls-Royce Spiritualists should bring with us when we arise in the morning until we go to bed at night. This is the 'orientation' we should bring with us that transcends any other orientation, sexual or otherwise, we may have when we become aware another person has come into our lives or crosses our path. Remember, whatever you do to love your neighbors should begin with feelings that perceive those neighbors as kin-folks. This is the *identity love* that St. Paul put first in his list of fruit of the Holy Spirit.

IDENTITY LOVE IS A FEELING

As a closing comment on *Identity Love* I would like to unpack a comment I have made more than once, namely, that Love is a feeling. Feelings (sometimes called emotions or attitudes) are one of the three aspects of behavior that lead to actions—those human behaviors we actually observe. The three are (1) feelings, (2) thoughts and (3) words. Thus, feelings lead to thoughts; thoughts lead to words; words lead to actions. Feelings are pre-conscious or sub-conscious attitudes that are like diving boards—they are springs to action. We assume them. We don't automatically call them by name or admit we have them at the time.

LOVE

In the case of the Good Samaritan[10] we are only told about his loving actions. In fact when Jesus told the parable, it was in a discussion about the meaning of the second great commandment—"Love your neighbor as yourself." Jesus did not address what love was in terms of feelings, thoughts, or words. Jesus only spoke about love as an act—what the Samaritan did, his behavior. But I am confident that the Samaritan acted on the basis of loving emotions he brought with him These feeling provoked him to say to some words (e.g 'How can I help you?') that directed his movement off the road toward the suffering man. So, love is a feeling that arises toward another person or persons who enter our field of awareness (through sight, sound, touch, or taste).

The Good Samaritan saw; he felt identity love; he acted lovingly. What was true of the Samaritan can be true of us. 'Love' is, first of all, a set of feelings we have that can provoke certain thoughts that we express in decisions we make and that result in observable behaviors.

A MODEL FOR HOW IDENTITY LOVE CAN WORK

I hope we all agree that the basic type of feeling that is needed in our love of our neighbor is *identity love*—the conviction that everyone we meet is truly a brother or sister. But is the concept of *identity love* adequate for giving us the practical advice we need for how such love works? Since Jesus gave us no guidance on this matter, I would like to suggest a possible model of how *identity love* might actually work for us in daily life. The three elements to the way *identity love feelings* might work are: Awareness, Appreciation and Affirmation.

Using the Samaritan as a Model:

First, he became *Aware* of all the people he saw on the road. Neither the scenery that surrounded him nor the press of his business

10. Luke 10:33ff.

preoccupied him. People were most important. He was open to other human beings that might come into his vision or his hearing. He probably looked at other people in-the-eye, said hello, or smiled as a way of saying, "I know you are there."

Second, he *Appreciated* them. He experienced each person as his brother or sister. He had a warm appreciative feeling that they, like himself, were attempting to live life with purpose and meaning. By no means did he judge them as either good or bad. He just felt they were on life's journey just as he was.

Third, he *Affirmed* a willingness to become involved and spend time, energy, and resource in helping them should they have a need. While he would offer assistance, he would not force himself upon others. Yet, he would not wait to take a place alongside a person should there be a major problem

These are three practical steps in the emotion *Identity Love* that the Good Samaritan might have felt as he knelt to help the man who fell among thieves along the Jericho Road. They are worth our consideration as we, too, seek to clarify what it might look like to love our neighbors in the modern world. Remember, we are talking about pre-conscious 'feelings'—not conscious thoughts. Thoughts follow feeling. Feelings are like diving boards. They are springboards to action. In this case of the 'good' Samaritan these feelings led to thoughts; and those thoughts led to words; and words led to actions. So it can be for us, too.

FEELINGS CAN BE TRAINED

Some of you might respond that The 3 A model sounds nice but how can you made it work since you claim that we are unaware of feelings; supposedly they just *are*? This is a good question. I have become convinced that feelings can be trained. Our feelings are not automatically at the mercy of past experience or the temptations of self-centeredness. We can take control of them. I have been influenced by the studies of J.D. Meyer and Peter

LOVE

Salovey[11], who have developed the idea of emotional intelligence. He is convinced that, while our emotions function pre-consciously and operate without thought, they can be trained back-handedly through our intentions. If our intentions are that we will let love of others dominate and control our feelings reflexively and without consideration in the moment, we can train our emotions to do so. I would like to suggest a training regime for influencing our emotional intelligence.

This training regime is based on the presumption that most of the habits of our daily lives stem from feelings that at one time or another in our pasts began with self-conscious trial-and-error acts that made us feel good. So, if we want *identity love* of others to become habitual—something that we eventually do automatically, without forethought—then we will need to practice it intentionally at first (through, for example, forcing ourselves to consciously enact the three As of Aware, Appreciate, and Affirm in specific interactions). But this is not enough, as most of us have found with New Year's resolutions. Something more is required.

The something more is keeping a Win Journal. We need to choose a person or a group who is willing to have us share with them on a regular basis. What we share is of critical importance. We should only share our victories, not our defeats; those interactions where we succeeded in *identity love* rather than the times when we forgot or failed. Because we tend to acquire habits that make us feel good (i.e., that please us) over time we can expect those feelings to work their way automatically back into our daily life. Hale-Evans has called this "Hacking our Brains.[12]"

I predict that this approach would help us move forward in our efforts to attain Rolls-Royce Spirituality. I turn next to a consideration of the most important determinant in making *identity love* become a reality, i.e., *self-control*.

---

11. Meyer & Salovey, *Emotional intelligence*, 202.
12. Hale-Evans, *Mind Performance Hacks*, 2.

3

SELF-CONTROL
The Foundation Fruit

I HAVE CALLED SELF-CONTROL the Foundation Fruit. By this I mean that nothing gets done without it! Self-control *controls* the rest of the fruit. Without self-control, *identity love* cannot even get off the ground. Much less will any of the actual behaviors of *identity love* (joy, peace, patience, kindness, generosity, faithfulness, and gentleness) ever be observed. The 'self' in Self-Control is the key because one's self resides at the core of every human being. Whatever else being created in God's image may mean awareness of oneself is certainly a central uniqueness of all human beings. Human selves, alone in all creation can, like God, consciously make decisions and determine the outcome of their lives.

We know that the self is forming in children the first time they use the pronoun 'I' in a sentence. When we hear them say, "I want cereal" or "I don't want to go to bed" or "I like Mary" or "I am cold," we know that a self is coming into being. This development of the self in human beings leads to identity and desire. In the past philosophers have called this 'vitalism' or 'the mind' as if to say the development of the self seems to be an inevitable force leading to a conscious awareness that transcends biological functioning. Plato described the self as a chariot rider that directs the impulses of the horse towards winning races that would lead to prizes and honors. In this case, the horse stood for all those natural impulses and passions that our selves control as we develop an identity in life. St. Paul suggests that control of those selves plays a crucial role in the expression of spirituality.

JESUS: SELF-DENIAL; PAUL: SELF CONTROL

It is interesting that while Jesus called for his followers to *deny* themselves in three of the four gospels (Matthew 16:24, Mark 8:34, Luke 9:23), Paul only calls for self-*control*. I wonder if Jesus would have changed his mind had he been thinking more of what was needed to be Christian among his followers who no longer saw him face-to-face. Paul did not call for self-denial or self-rejection. In fact, I think he knew that to follow the commandment to love the neighbor as oneself[13] one had to start with '*self* love.' Here Jesus might have intuitively agreed with Paul because Jesus affirmed the age-old admonition to love our neighbor *as ourselves*. Self-love gives us the understanding of what it might mean to love others. It is where we start in our efforts to practice Rolls-Royce Spirituality.

Becoming aware of, but controlling, our own self-love as we attempt to love others is a crucial first step. Self-Control is the *How* while joy, peace, patience, kindness, generosity, faithfulness, and gentleness are the *Whats* of *identity love*. These are what love looks like in human action. These are the exact ways we tend to love ourselves! We are joyful peaceful, patient, kind, generous faithful, and gentle with ourselves. And these are the ways we should love others. When the old song claims, "They will know we are Christian by our love," this list of specific behaviors is what people see and how we act toward ourselves.

13. Mark 12:13.

But others will never see these behaviors unless we control our selves. This is an indisputable fact, not a fleeting fantasy. In a sense, controlling our self-love while loving others is a paradox. However, loving ourselves can become a self-conscious model for us as to what it means to love others. The problem remains: we will never be able to love others unless at the same time we exert some control over loving ourselves. Lest this sound like double-talk, let's reflect on the way that self-love, more often than not, becomes the dominant role we play in life. Controlling the self in order to love others is no simple task.

SELF DEVELOPMENT

Erik Erikson proposed a model of self-development that is worthy of consideration. He called it a step-wise plan for "ego" development (ego being his synonym for self). He suggested that development of the "self" could be conceived as following eight stages from infancy to old age. In each stage, the self faces a different kind of crisis. If the crisis is resolved successfully, the self moves on to the next stage. A summary of the model is as follows:

Age Crisis Resolution

    Infancy to 18 months Trust versus Mistrust Hope, Drive

    18 months to 3 years Autonomy versus Shame Self-Control, Courage, Will

    3–5 years Initiative versus Guilt Purpose

    6–12 years Industry versus Inferiority Competence

    12–18 years Identity & Solidarity vs. Role Confusion Fidelity

    18–35 (Young Adulthood) Intimacy versus Isolation Love

    25–55 (Middle Adulthood) Generativity versus Stagnation Care

    55–65 yrs. (Later Adulthood) Integrity versus Despair Wisdom[14]

---

14. Erikson, *Identity*, 51ff.

This is a helpful insight into how human 'selves' evolve over a lifetime within western culture. The model is an astute combination of physical ability, family nurturance, and cultural expectations. At its extreme, however, it could produce a narcissistic, self-centered individual who knows how to work the system and ends life with satisfaction that is grounded in personal achievement and close family relationships—i.e., self-lovable incarnate! The only self-control in such a model is personally motivated to increase one's self-esteem. At no point, except possibly during middle adulthood where pride is taken in bringing new life into the world, do we see anything like altruism, much less identity love of others.

Interestingly, while Erikson's model is a fairly accurate model for understanding normal self-development, it could be judged to be a good example of how self-love can stand in the way of love for others. Self-control is not mentioned as a virtue to be desired at any of life's stages. The struggle that comes in seeking to avoid failure in each of Erikson's ego crises results in self-hate, not self-control. We are still left with no sense of how self-control enters into the expression of *identity love* through the spiritual fruit Paul lists in his letter to the Galatians.

This observation poses a quandary for us as we think of the role of the self in expressing identity love and its derivatives—joy, peace, kindness, generosity, etc. How can we honor the normal development of the self as grounded in God's good creation, yet control the self in a manner that honor's God's redemptive will as seen in fruit of the spirit? This has been a recurring dilemma in modern Christian psychology as it has dealt with depressed persons who needed to increase their love of themselves but at the same time temper the self-centeredness that sometimes occurs. Self-control is appropriate but how can it be achieved?

THE SELF AND SITUATIONAL STRESS

Perhaps a greater danger to self-control than the possibility of becoming too prideful, as in Erkison's model, is the response of our selves to the frustration of situational stress. In an earlier volume[15], I noted that Sigmund Freud, the well-known psychoanalyst, suggested that stress in life resulted from three sources: personal limitations, the reality of the physical world, and the behavior of other people. I would add a fourth: cultural expectations.

Personal limitations are those stresses that result, for example, from our inability to remain alert 24 hours in a row, go to work when we have the flu, lift the rock that has fallen on the highway, comprehend enough information to pass a test, or remember the names of everybody in our group. These kinds of situations frustrate us.

The reality of the physical world are those stresses that result, for example, from being homesick when our army unit is based overseas, from a fog preventing our plane to take off, from a computer breaking down as we are typing a term paper, or from a stoplight turning red when we are in a hurry. These kinds of situations frustrate us.

The behavior of other people are those stresses that arise, for example, when another driver suddenly cuts in front of us in traffic, when our child suddenly misbehaves at school, when neighbors fail to keep their yard clean, when a teenager plays loud music late into the night, when we get in an argument with our boss at work, when our baggage is lost at the airport, or when we come to an impasse with someone we love. These kinds of situations frustrate us.

The expectations of our culture are those stresses that result, for example, when a teenager is not chosen to be on the cheerleading squad, when a company downsizes and a job is lost, when a divorcee is embarrassed at family gatherings, when a student has to quit school because of excess debt, when a graduate student fails to make a grade, or when we are ticketed for over-parking just as we come back to our car. These cultural expectations frustrate us.

---

15. Malony, *When Getting Along Seeems Impossible*, 32ff.

SUCCESSES, PROBLEMS, CONFLICTS

Of course, all these frustrating, stressful situations can range from peccadilloes to major struggles. One way to think of the various situations we face in life is to conceive of them as one of three kinds: successes, problems, or conflicts.

Successes are those situations in life where we meet no opposition of any kind and achieve the goal to which we were aspiring. An example of *success* would be that rare person who had mastered each of Erikson's ego-crises and had reached later adulthood with a feeling of absolute integrity—the sense that life is good; that if s/he had the chance to live life all over again, they would change nothing. Their lives would be full of successes. It goes without saying that this is an ideal state and very, very few people reach this pinnacle.

Problems are those life situations where opposition to one's ambitions, goals, and endeavors are experienced in one or more of the areas discussed above. Problems require reason and effort for the resistance to be overcome but in the average life, most problems can be resolved through adaptation or compromise. Problem solving can be hard work but it results in the reduction of stress. Most people learn a variety of ways to redirect, substitute, try again, circumnavigate, share, delay, cooperate, or change.

Conflicts are another matter. These are those major struggles in which a persons' psychic existence—their very selves—are threatened. Like major physical operations, scars result and stress rarely fully disappears. One way to look at conflict is to say that we don't *have* conflicts; we *go into* conflict. Experiencing conflict is like being in an earthquake. The very foundation of our sense of self resembles the earth moving under our feet. We fight to survive. We fantasy there is no hope. We feel we will not and cannot make our way through. We fight for our lives, both figuratively and literally.

Were we to picture life in terms of a bell-curve, successes and conflicts would be the tails on each end and problems would dominate. This is where most of us spend our time. Problem solving reflects our efforts to handle the stress of life and manage our self-esteem. The Self-control Paul calls for in Galatians 5 would probably be easier to achieve in the middle of the bell-curve while each of the tails (Success and Conflict) would find it more difficult. The danger of the Success life would be Self-Aggrandizement (cf. the Rich Young Ruler in Luke 10:29ff) while the danger of the Conflict life would be Self-Depreciation (cf. the crippled man who waited so long to be put in the pool of Siloam in John 5:7ff). I suppose most readers would agree that a life without stress is almost improbable, but possible, while a life dominated entirely by stress is possible, but improbable.

SELF-CONTROL AND FAITH

I have come to believe that the answer to the Self-Control Paul recommends may be simpler, yet more profound, than one might think. Could it not be that the intentional self-control St. Paul included toward the end of his list of spiritual fruit comes only after an experience with the Risen Christ and the indwelling of God's Holy Spirit? This may be functionally simple but deeply profound! This may be the place where St. Paul's self-control and Jesus' self-denial come together. Jesus' admonition in Mark is worthy of reconsideration because it addresses the achievement of strong self-identity included in Erikson's model and offers promise to those whose life feel hopeless:

He called the crowd with his disciples and said to them, "If any want to follow me let them DENY (sic) themselves and take up their cross and follow me. For those who want to save their life will lose it, and those who lose their life for my sake, and for the sake of the gospel, will save it."[16]

This seems to be a clear illustration of intentional self-control for the sake of a higher reason—namely attaining Rolls-Royce Spirituality. Only the example and teaching of Jesus and the inspirational guidance of the Holy Spirit make possible the type of

---

16. Mark 8:34–35.

control of self-love that results in being joyful peaceful, patient, kind, generous faithful, and gentle in our love of other human beings. Such self-control requires a conscious decision coupled with an openness to direction that only the Holy Spirit can provide. Such an experience can be the key to Rolls-Royce Spirituality and the transcendence of mundane faith. It is this type of modern miracle that can lead us to affirm with the conviction that God's kingdom is alive and present in human life.

With this in mind, we turn next to a separate consideration of each of the practical expressions of spiritual fruit mentioned in Galatians 5. Remember that they will each only be possible with the type of Self-Control we have been discussing as a foundation for our behavior. What I said earlier is worth repeating as an introduction. I stated earlier that "Self-Control is the *How* while joy, peace, patience, kindness, generosity, faithfulness, and gentleness are the *Whats* of *identity love*. These are what love looks like in human action."

We will consider next the first overt behavior that Paul includes in his list of the fruit of the Holy Spirit—*Joy*.

4

JOY
The Mood Fruit

I HAVE LABELED *Joy* the Mood fruit. *Joy* should not be confused with *Enjoy* or *Rejoice*. *Joy* is located much deeper in the psyche than either of these. *Enjoy* implies a conscious delight in something that happens—like a favorite food that one eats or a new movie one sees. You usually share what you enjoy—as in saying, "Um that was delicious," or "Wow, that was an exciting plot in that movie." *Rejoice*, too, is more conscious than *joy*—like when someone says to you, "I'll bet you're rejoiced to finally see your daughter graduate from college," or when the pastor says, "Let us rejoice on this Easter Sunday." All three of them (*joy, enjoy,* and *rejoice*) are first cousins, but Paul chose *joy* instead of the other two in his list of spiritual fruit for a reason. I think I have probably intuited a bit of his reasoning in labeling *joy* a mood fruit—meaning something that is real but sub-conscious, yet something that can be observed and felt by others. Thus, moods have both an internal and an external meaning.

JOY

Before we explore Paul's thinking further, let me tell you about two persons in whom I have experienced joy. I think they will provide examples of why Paul listed *joy* right after *love*. The first example is a secretary with whom I worked for much of my career and the second is the woman to whom I been married for nearly sixty years. Both of them have exuded *joy*.

MARNIE

Marnie was the executive secretary of Fuller Seminary's School of Psychology in which I taught for over 35 years. From the first moment in the late 1960s when she welcomed my family into Pasadena on a sweltering July day after an exhausting car trip across country, Marnie was upbeat, cheerful, and affirming. In all the years after that day she remained the same—happy, smiling, cheerful, and optimistic. The weather did not seem to matter. Smog, rain, wind, sunshine—they were all the same to her. Family stress did not seem to dampen her mood, either. Her husband suffered premature debilitating hearing loss and her daughters had some troubles growing up. Through it all, her joy did not abate. As I stopped by her desk in the morning, she was looking up at me from her busy desk and complimented something about my appearance or behavior. She would say, "That's a nice tie," or "You look ready for class," or "Isn't this a beautiful day?" She was joy-filled. During her years of service, she was the personal secretary to the founding dean and involved in all the stress that goes into establishing a new school. She remained a joy-filled Can-Do person. She retired some years ago. Her retirement celebration was an event to be remembered by the many who shared the experience of her joy—students and faculty alike!

SUZANNA

Suzanna is my wife of sixty years. We met and courted in college and have experienced the typical list of positive and negative events of married life. From the very first days after our wedding I noticed a characteristic I have come to treasure—she wakes up full of joy. I don't mean giddy or laughing, just joyful. It is a similar mood that I once saw illustrated on a poster. It pictured the back of a young infant running on the beach toward the water. The by-line stated these words: "The world and I have met each other and we are in love." That is Suzanna! Of course, she can get worried, incensed, angry, defensive, and sad like any other person, but she always begins every day as if it was a brand new opportunity for solving problems, accomplishing tasks, and healing hurts. She has been so constant in that ability that I have become accustomed to it and expect it. However, I never cease to marvel at her joy. Even with the personal trials associated with physical breakdowns in a now 80 year old woman, she has maintained her joy. She continues to greet each new day with optimism and expectation. Like Marnie, Suzanna is a Can-Do person and I am grateful for sharing in her joy.

Both Marnie and Suzanna brought (and bring) a mood of *joy* with them into each day of their lives. I am not sure that either of them would have admitted that this was what they were doing. It was just what they did. It was definitely an attitude that came out of their sub-conscious. But remember I said that a mood had external effect as well as internal meaning. I was, and have been, very aware of the effect of their *joy* mood on me. I don't think I ever said, "Are you aware of what your *joy* mood does to me?" I take that back, I may have mentioned to Suzanna how pleased I was that she always woke up so joyful—but only now and then. My memory was she said replied, "I'm glad you like it; let's have breakfast." The external effect of both her's and Marnie's mood of *joy* has afforded me many pleasant memories.

THE SOURCE OF JOY

My question is "Where did their *joy* come from?" I have a best-guess answer that fits in well with our conviction about the work of the Holy Spirit. Marnie was a Christian until she died. Suzanna remains a faithful Christian. I believe that long ago each of them allowed the Holy Spirit to open their hearts up to the truth that great joy could come into their lives if they affirmed that they had been chosen by God to participate in His attempt to create a community of love and peace and justice on this earth. Further, their joy has worked its way deep below their consciousness as they have allowed Jesus Christ to redeem and reclaim them for this role in life. As the periods of their lives have come and gone, they have trusted in Almighty God for the future may hold. Thus, the mood of *joy* was born and developed over time until *joy* became second nature to both of them.

This is what Paul would intend for those who aspire to Rolls-Royce Spirituality. Joy is the ideal subconscious mood that should underlie all efforts to express the rest of the fruit of the Spirit. In fact, trying to make peace, evidence patience, be kind and generous, remain faithful, and be gentle will be experienced as a sham without a joyous mood. Perhaps we should remind ourselves of the best mood-motto in the Bible: "This is the day that the Lord has made, let us rejoice and be glad in it."[17] "Rejoice" means a renewal of "Joy"—Joy does not come naturally as one observes the evil all about; it is a renewal of joy based on faith in God that results in a decision of how to live within each day.

THE COURAGE TO BE—A DECISION THAT OVERCOMES DESPAIR

The late existentialist theologian, Paul Tillich, wrote a book entitled *The Courage to Be* that deals with this leap of faith that led to joy in both Marnie's and Suzanna's lives. While they had both made the decision to join God in kingdom building, neither of their lives was free from distress. Health problems had plagued them personally and they were both alert to the difficulty of seeing any evidence that the world's evil was being overcome. Further, they were well-educated individuals who were well-aware of

---

17. Psalm 118:24.

arguments against religious belief in God—much less in the Risen Christ. Yet they had made the decision to live by faith.

Tillich's understanding of faith fits Marnie and Suzanna well. He suggests that affirming Christian faith in the modern world is like persons taking a mountain hike and coming to the edge of a cliff where the path ends. Seeing that the path takes up again on another cliff across a deep chasm from where they are standing, they realize they will have to jump. They become afraid they cannot make it. They feel a panic rising up. They feel desperate. Tillich calls this a "sickness unto death." They seriously consider turning back and going home. They wish there was an easier way. Tillich contends there is no easier way. People have to take "a leap of faith that God is at work." Both Marnie and Suzanna have taken that *leap of faith*. Faith is a decision—it leads to Joy. But it is an illusion to think the decision is easy or that the *Joy* that faith brings is but a passing fantasy. No, faith's Joy is a deep-seated conviction God is alive and well and very present in the world today.[18]

As Hebrews 11:1 (NRSV) states so convincingly, *"faith is, indeed, the assurance of things hoped for and the evidence of things not seen."*[19] Faith means living 'as if' it is so. Sigmund Freud wrote his critique of religious faith in the volume entitled *The Future of an Illusion*. The book was his critique of religious faith. He felt it was infantile and neurotic—an illusion. The Swiss psychoanalyst and Reform pastor, Oskar Pfister, wrote a review of Freud's book entitled "The Illusion of the Future" defending religion. Freud really meant that religion was a "delusion," (meaning a fantasy—completely false) not an "illusion" (meaning a vision of a future ideal).[20] Pfister used the word "illusion" in the same sense that Hebrews wrote of faith as the assurance of things hoped for, the conviction of things not seen.[21] Pfister was convinced that religious faith was the only "illusion" that had a future. His was an argument in favor of the leap of faith that provides the foundation for the fruit

---

18. Tillich, *The Courage to Be*, 162.
19. Hebrews 11:1.
20. Freud, *The Future of an Illusion*, 5.
21. Pfister, *The illusion of the future*.

of JOY that is a part of Rolls-Royce Spirituality. As Issac Watts' well-known Christmas hymn proclaims *Joy to the world, the Lord is come; let earth receive her king.*[22]

---

22. Watts, "Joy to the World" in *The United Methodist Hymnal*, 246.

5

PEACE
The Referee Fruit

PEACE IS THE FRUIT that has many implications for a variety of situations—both personal and interpersonal. The word can be bantered around differently. For example, we can be *at peace, peaceful, peace -makers, receivers of peace, offer peace, declare peace,*—likely all in the same day! My choice of the phrase 'the Referee Fruit' probably applies most to the task of *peace making.* That may be a good place to start but not a complete place to finish.

As Jesus said in the Beatitudes "Blessed are the peacemakers, for they will be called the children of God."[23] And so they are, because God, their father, is in the business of peace. Paul states it well toward the end of his second letter to the Corinthians by proclaiming ". . .live in peace; and the God of love and peace be with you."[24] In both situations, making peace and living in peace,

---

23. Matthew 5:9.
24. 2 Cor 12:11b.

Rolls-Royce Spiritualists are called to be a 'referee'—to put themselves in-between situations and resolve conflictual situations.

PEACE AND DISTRESS

I think it would be helpful to see if we can agree on some working definitions of 'peace' and its opposite 'distress.' I think this might help us better understand the role of 'peace making—a central component of being a good 'referee.'

Earlier, I mentioned a model of the three life situations that we all face at one time or another: i.e., success, stress, and distress.[25] However, I did not clearly distinguish between 'problems' that cause us stress and 'conflicts' that provoke distress. In fact, I believe 'conflict' is a state of mind (*distress*) rather than a type of situation (like problems) that we solve by negotiation, compromise, or change of plans. We go *into conflict* when we feel that there is no hope of solving a problem coupled with a sense that our self-esteem is in danger of attack, or even annihilation. This state of mind is called *distress*. When we are *distressed* we feel so threatened that we have to defend ourselves or surrender to other peoples' power over us when we don't really mean it. This is known as the "fight/flight syndrome." A helpful way to imagine going into conflict (i.e., experiencing distress) is to think of it like an earthquake in which we feel the ground shake beneath our feet and we are panicked that we will fall. Conflict calls for drastic fight or flight reactions.

Some helpful couplets make these distinctions clearer:

- Problems are differences to be resolved; Conflicts are feelings to be reduced;
- Better to say *people go into conflict* than to say *people have a conflict*;
- We reduce the distress of conflict in order to return to problem solving;

---

25. Malony, *When getting along seems impossible*: 33.

- Peace is not the absence of stress, but the feeling that one can handle situations when they arise.
- Peace feelings are the opposite of Conflict feelings.

What I am describing is illustrated during war time. Laura Hillenbrand's book titled *Unbroken*[26] tells about the life of Louis Zamperini, track star of the 1936 Olympics who subsequently became a Japanese POW in World War II. She describes vividly his distressed state of mind. His feelings vacillated between aggressive excitement as he saw US bombs destroy buildings on Japan-held islands and his utter panic as he fled to safety when his plane went down and he was captured by Japanese after forty days on a life raft. On the one hand he was motivated to fight with abandon while on the other hand he was fleeing for his life. Of course, he had a third option: he could have floated a white flag of surrender and become a prisoner of war—which is exactly what he did in the end! He was distressed and in conflict. He spent several years in Japanese prisons—all equally abusive and life-threatening.

Being in conflict (i.e., Distressed) is like war—pure and simple. While Zamperini's example is extreme, it is, nevertheless, illustrative of what happens in interpersonal relations—again and again. Often, we can see distress in divorce, in family discord, in neighborhood differences, in car accidents, among different religions, and in child and marital abuse.

Now I think that *peace* is the opposite of conflict. Peace, like conflict, is a state of mind. But in contrast to the distress of conflict feelings that lead to panic reactions, peace feelings lead to calming and soothing responses. Being *at* peace means being *out of* conflict.

Peace making, then, could be conceived as a process of *reducing* conflictual and *increasing* peaceful states of mind. Yet another way of looking at conflict reduction is to say that it enhances problem solving. Often when folks feel at peace are they willing to work on a solution to whatever it was that provoked the conflict emotions to rise up in the beginning.

---

26. Hillenbrand, *Unbroken*.

Let's assume you agree with my definitions enough to be willing to turn to the *making of peace* for that is the gift-of-the-Spirit that Paul includes in his Galatians 5 list. Peace making would seem to be a very important skill to those who would aspire to Rolls-Royce Spirituality.

PEACE MAKING IS A GIFT OF THE SPIRIT

Initially, and probably most importantly, it is crucial to note that *peace making* is a spiritual gift. Saying peace is a 'spiritual' gift is one of those statements my wife might respond to with "Duh" (her way of saying any fool knows that. She would add, "After all that is what your whole book is about."). And she might be right in one sense because all the other chapters are labeled with one of the gifts-of-the-Spirit. However, each of the other gifts have modern practical counterparts that provoke us to start discussion of them with some understanding, as minimal as that might be. Any counselor, who has tried to work with folk who are in conflict, knows how difficult it is. It's like wading into a foggy stream with little knowledge or plan for how to get across to the other side. At least, that has been my experience. Relying on the Holy Spirit for guidance is both a crucial and necessary process in becoming a peace maker.

We probably need no reminding that the Holy Spirit is the Spirit of God the Father *and* God the Son. And it is the Son, Jesus our Lord, who proclaimed the profound truth when he said to His disciples (and to us), *"Peace I leave with you; my peace I give to you. I do not give to you as the world gives. Do not let your heart be troubled, and do not let them be afraid."*[27]

And what is this 'peace' that only God, through Jesus and the Holy Spirit, can give to those who are in conflict . . . whose hearts are troubled . . . who are afraid? It is a truth that speaks to the basic experience of conflict, i.e., that one's very survival is in danger. It is the reassurance that one will survive! . . . that one's psychic value is not in danger! . . . that one is treasured and valued and loved! . . .

27. John 14:27.

that one is precious in the eyes of God!... that one is safe! This is the root meaning of the best known verse in the whole Bible, John 3:16, *"For God so loved the world that He gave His only son; that whosoever believes in Him should not perish but have everlasting life."*[28]

Whatever else this verse should mean in terms of life after death, in this present life it means that there should be no fear of *dying* here and now in this frightful situation. This life can be lived in the confidence that one's self-confidence and self-esteem and ultimate value has been assured *if* one puts one's faith in the God and father of our Lord Jesus Christ. Through Christ's death and resurrection the fact of God's everlasting love for each of us has been demonstrated at all times, in every place, and for each circumstance. When Jesus said on the cross "It is finished" He stated that His work for us had been done. As Paul proclaimed in Romans 8:

Who will separate us from the love of Christ? Will hardship, or distress, or persecution, or famine, or nakedness, or peril or sword? ...No, in all these things we are more than conquerors through him who loved us. For I am convinced that neither death, nor life, nor angels nor rulers, nor things present, nothings to come, nor powers, nor height, nor depth, nor anything else in all creation will be able to separate us from the love of Christ Jesus our Lord.[29]

Wow! A better definition of what it means to have a peace-filled state of mind could not be found! Don't you agree? At a recent Sunday morning worship service at the church I attend, we had a visible demonstration of the father welcoming the younger brother home in Jesus' parable of the Prodigal Son. A saucer of oil was given to the person at the end of every pew with the instruction to turn to the person next to them and state as they anointed the top of their hand, "You are love, You are precious, You are accepted by God." Every person at church that day was reminded of God's love and care irrespective of whatever distress they might have been experiencing.

28. John 3:16.
29. Vs.35 39.

PEACE

Now, I can just hear somebody complaining, "How do we know that everyone who was anointed that Sunday was a person who had put their faith in God?" We don't, but it doesn't matter. As the late theologian, Karl Barth, reportedly responded when asked, "What is the difference between those in the church and out of the church?" *No difference. Both are loved by Almighty God as seen in Jesus Christ. Those in the church know it. Those outside the church don't yet know it.*

Peace Making, therefore, is the skill of reminding old Christians as well as the skill of introducing not-yet Christians to the truth of God's everlasting love. Awareness of this truth in the time of conflictual emotions can result in a peaceful state of mind. As the old saying states, "It will work; check it out." Christians aspiring to Rolls-Royce Spirituality should depend on the Holy Spirit to help reinstate this truth of God's love in themselves as they share the same truth with others they are trying to help.

Earlier I mentioned Hillenbrand's book on the experience of Louis Zamperini who became a Japanese POW during World War II. He was in prison for over two years. During this time he was subjected to extreme cruelty by a guard nicknamed "the Bird." When he returned to southern California after the war, he became consumed with returning to Japan, finding "Bird," and killing him. He became alcoholic as he could not ever seem to make enough money to make the trip. Yet his nightmares of memory and his obsession with murdering "Bird" for what he suffered continued to plague him.

In the midst of his continuing turmoil, he reluctantly agreed to go to a Billy Graham tent meeting where his wife, Cynthia, had had a religious experience. He refused to participate in the meeting but became alert as Graham described Jesus teaching and His rising from the dead. He felt judged by Graham's description of drowning men who need a Savior but he left before accepting the offer of salvation. He went to another meeting just to please Cynthia. His mind was muddled with all the pain he had suffered. He tried to leave the meeting but became convicted. He turned and

Rolls-Royce Spirituality

walked down to the front and received the salvation being offered by Graham. The end result of this true story is that he was freed from his compulsion to kill "Bird" and later he journeyed to Japan to try to meet with him and offer reconciliation.[30] A better illustration of peace-making and peace-fulfillment would be hard to find.

PEACE MAKING BEGINS WITH THE PEACE MAKER

I have a confession to make—I don't know any ready-to-apply peace making skills, although, as a clinical psychologist and pastoral counselor, I have been in numerous peace making situations. Nor do I make any claims to having been overly successful in these endeavors. By I, like hopefully you the reader, are on a pilgrimage to attain Rolls-Royce Spirituality and I know one thing for certain—peace makers must be *at peace themselves* or all their efforts will be in vain. This is a truth that cannot be denied as much as we like to claim we are but vulnerable human beings ourselves. Personally, I have found *peace* again and again as I reaffirmed what the theologian Paul Tillich claimed is the basic truth of the gospel—namely, *you are accepted*. I have found his words about the grace of God to be insightful. I share them now as a statement of how the Holy Spirit can inspire those of us who hope to be helpful in our peace making by becoming at peace ourselves.

> "Sometimes. . .a wave of light breaks into our darkness, and it is as if a voice were saying: 'You are accepted. You are accepted by that which is greater than you, and the name of which you do not know. Do not ask for the name now, perhaps you will find it later. Do not try to do anything now; perhaps later you will do much. Do not seek for anything, do not perform anything; do not intend anything. Simply accept the fact that you are accepted! If that happens to us, we experience grace. . . In that moment, grace conquers sin, and reconciliation bridges the gulf of

---

30. Hillenbrand, *Unbroken*.

estrangement. . .In the light of this grace we perceive the power of grace in our relations to others and to ourselves.[31]

I believe these words parallel the truth of John 14:27ff where Jesus proclaims, *"Peace I leave with you; my peace I give to you. I do not give to you as the world gives. Do not let your hearts be troubled, and do not let them be afraid."*[32]

These are the true words from the Holy Spirit to all those who would exude Rolls-Royce Spirituality.

---

31. Tillich, *The Shaking of the Foundations*, 162.
32. John 14:27ff.

6

PATIENCE
The Fisherman Fruit

I LABELED PATIENCE AS the fisherman fruit because if there is one thing a good fisherman learns to do it is to be patient and to wait on the fish to bite. Interestingly, this patient waiting of fishermen is embedded in long-practiced skills of anticipation and achievement. So it is with the spiritual fruit of *patience*: it is embedded within the Christian faith and hope. The patient waiting in Rolls-Royce Spirituality knows in its heart the absolute truth of the Eucharistic proclamation "Christ has died, Christ is risen, Christ will come again."[33]

There is a somewhat dated joke about the day-to-day practice of Christian patience that provides an example of why St. Paul included *patience* in his list of spiritual fruit. It seems as if a car was stopped by a policeman shortly after following a line of traffic through a stoplight. "Why did you stop me, officer?" the driver asked after showing the officer proof that he had a license and that

---

33. *The United Methodist Book of Worship*, 38.

he owned the car. "I don't think I ran a red light and I know I was not speeding." "Well," the officer replied, "I assumed you had stolen this car since I noticed that Christian symbol on your bumper and you honked your horn so persistently and leaned out your window and shouted at the car ahead of you when his motor died and he was slow in getting his car started again. I couldn't believe a Christian would act like that."

I would guess that it would be fairly common for people to assume that Christians would not be so impatient that they would make a scene when cars ahead of them in traffic did not move fast enough. But many Christians would agree that patient automobile driving was not necessarily a valid assumption in many situations. Patience is often more a wish than a reality and Christians are often as guilty as any other group of such discourtesies. Nevertheless, such impatience as seen in the incident recounted above does reflect the more serious concern we should address in our aspirations toward Rolls-Royce Spirituality. It could reflect depth substitution of practical, mundane affairs for the really-real world of patient waiting for the kingdom of God that is breaking into human existence.

PATIENCE IN THE OLD TESTAMENT

It is fascinating that *patience* is not mentioned in the Old Testament except for a few verses in the Psalms. However, the forty year trek from Egypt to the Promised Land is fraught with examples of Hebrew 'impatience' over the hardship and length of the journey. Again and again, God is pictured as frustrated and angry with their lack of trust that they will ever get to the Promised Land to which Moses claims God is leading them. They complain bitterly and even insinuate that God has abandoned them. They compare their hardships to the good times they experienced as Pharaoh's slaves in Egypt.

But that is just the issue: in Egypt they were slaves who had no land. They had no hope. From that day to this, when the going gets rough, people can be tempted to give in to *immediate gratification* and prefer some condition not nearly as good if they had waited and trusted in *delayed gratification*. God had promised Abraham that his descendents would be given a land to call their own, but it had not yet happened. Although this dream was what prompted the Hebrews to follow Moses, doubts had arisen. They were ready to give up on God's promise. And how did God react? He was ready to give up on them but Moses pleaded with God to give the Hebrews one more chance. Moses hoped that God would be patient with their impatience!

THE MOSES ROLE

Perhaps it is the 'Moses role' that those aspiring to Rolls-Royce Spirituality should adopt. Patience was both a modeling and a mediating role for Moses. No doubt, he, like the other Hebrews, experienced that the trip from Egypt to Canaan was taking a long, long time. Yet Moses remained hopeful and true to his leadership responsibility. He did not falter. Although the dating is somewhat uncertain, Moses may have known of the prophet Isaiah's statement "...*they that wait on the Lord shall renew their strength; they shall mount with wings as eagles; they shall run and not be weary; they shall walk and not faint.*"[34]

Further, Moses did not claim special privilege—another dimension of patience. He, like every Hebrew, anticipated the day when they would receive the land. In Moses' case, however, it was not to be. God led Moses up Mt. Nebo to look over Canaan, the land just across the Jordan River that God has promised the Hebrews. You can just imagine the excitement Moses felt as he anticipated leading his followers in the conquest of Jericho. But God said, "You will not go. You will die here. Joshua will take your place." Though bitterly disappointed, Moses did not grumble or

---

34. Isa 40:31.

PATIENCE

beg God to change His mind. He accepted his fate and remained faithful to the end. Yes, Moses set a patient example both in his leadership and in his acceptance of a hope that did not come to pass.

Moses' life experience is worthy of following as a true spiritual fruit that can be applied today to those who experience delay in realizing their hopes or who have to adjust to hopes that never come to pass. I'm thinking of the boy who had to delay his dream of a college education when he had to work to support his mother after his father died. I am also thinking of the mother who foresaw her own death before either of her adult children married and fulfilled her long-held dream to be a grandmother.

Patience may seem like an insipid antidote to such folk. *Reassurance* or *Comfort* might be perceived as more helpful. But, in fact, *patience* could be conceived as including both of these. Certainly, both reassurance and comfort were included in Moses' patience experience in that it led him to never give up on God's promise to provide the Promised Land and the comfort he demonstrated in accepting God's decision that he would die without ever seeing that promise fulfilled.

This is the kind of patience essential to Rolls-Royce Spirituality. It is grounded in faith that God can be trusted to eventually establish his influence over all the world and that, in the meantime, each of us is destined to play a part in that process at this time, in this place, for ever how long we live. This is patience embedded in the fruit of the Holy Spirit. It is daily trust in God for the here and now as well as the there and then.

ERIKSON'S FINAL EGO-CRISIS—INTEGRITY

The psychoanalyst Erik Erikson, whose stages we mentioned earlier, concluded that the last ego crisis people face in life is a "Moses type" evaluation of their lives that leads them to have a sense of *integrity* or *despair*. One might think that for those folk who have achieved most of their goals in life, patience would be the last thing they would want. Many individuals have been Can-Do persons. They solved problems, worked hard, faced obstacles, loved deeply, had successful marriages, had children who made them proud, and grandchildren they indulged. I have a good friend who epitomizes this sense of life *integrity* as he has aged. He served with injury in the armed services, started his own business, weathered economic downfalls, earned a good living, and retired with his wife to a residential community where he plays golf every week and attends classes on photography. He is able to take a trip or two each year to new destinations. He has been successful. He can sing along with Frank Sinatra "I did it my way" and is impatient with others who do not try hard enough.

But those folk who have a number of unfinished dreams, failed endeavors, or frustrated relationships don't feel the same way. Despair could easily be what they are experiencing at this time in life. For these folk, patience might still be an option—but only if it were understood as a *gift of the Spirit*.

Thinking of the spiritual gift of patience as the opposite of despair requires some elaboration, however. The post-retirement years (called by some authors "the last third of life") should probably be split into two sections: (1) retirement and (2) late life. If persons live long enough, their mobility, strength, and health will diminish. It will happen to everyone regardless of whether they experienced integrity or despair during their retirement years. Patience becomes an option for everyone either because of success that flounders or success that never happened.

Jacques, the melancholy courtier in Shakespeare's "As You Like It" speaks of this late life period in those famous words about the last of the seven stages of life that he calls *second childishness* in which persons exist "sans too, sans eyes, sans taste, sans everything." Jacques contextualizes the description of second childishness with those famous words within a soliloquy that begins with those famous words: "All the world's a stage and all men and women merely players. They have their exits and their entrances and one man in his history plays many parts."[35] All of this is to say, *integrity* may have its limits if one lives long enough.

In a somewhat less lurid depiction, Jane Marie Thibault, co-author of the provocative book *Pilgrimage into the Last Third of Life: 7 Gateways to Spiritual Growth*[36] compared the last stage of life to entering a monastery. Monks live with people who are strangers, off to the side of what most people are doing with their daily lives. They take a vow of poverty and live in one-room cells. They eat simple food and give up the freedom to choose favorite foods. They surrender ownership of property and the enjoyment of physical comforts. Often, they commit themselves to stay in the same place for the rest of their lives and they give a leader at the monastery control over almost everything else.

She suggested that "what transpires naturally in later life corresponds to existence in a monastery. The lifestyle and practices of monastic life closely resemble the sensory interpersonal, psychological and material losses of later life. (If one lives long enough)

1. Personal, special relationships become fewer or even nonexistent due to death, relocation, sensory losses, and illness;
2. Beloved property must be relinquished, especially when moving into a retirement home;
3. Enjoyment of physical comforts and pleasures is diminished due to dietary restrictions, inability to digest foods, chronic pain
4. Obedience is required to the authority of the MD, RN, insurance plans, and over solicitous children;
5. Especially in nursing homes persons face loss of many freedoms: lack of control of time, diminished ability to change location, lack of privacy, loss of individuality and social marginalization."[37]

---

35. Shakespeare, As You Like It, Act II, Scene VII.
36. Thibault and Morgan, *Pilgrimage*, 116–117.
37. Ibid, 116–117.

JESUS TALKS TO PETER ABOUT THE END OF LIFE

Shakespeare's and Thibault's descriptions of late life are paralleled by the words of Jesus that appear at the very end of the Gospel of John. In this third resurrection appearance, Jesus is speaking to the disciples at the seashore and says to Peter after breakfast, *"..Very truly, I tell you, when you were younger, you used to fasten your own belt and to go wherever you wished. But when you grow old, you will stretch out your hands, and some else will fasten a belt around you and take you where you do not wish to go. . .Follow me."*[38]

Not Erikson and neither Shakespeare nor Thibault offer a resolution to the challenge of later life. Jesus does. He ends his description of what will happen to Peter if he lives long enough with the simple admonition, "Follow me." This is Hope. This is Gospel. This is Good News. The question remains, "How is it Good News to follow Peter in following Jesus when one is trying to care for oneself and barely holding on to life?" The answer to this question is deeply related to the gift of Patience and the effort to attain Rolls-Royce Spirituality.

The answer to following Jesus in later life lies at the heart of the spiritual gift of patience. A synonym for patience is "long suffering" and the temptation for Christians is to give up following Jesus and to doubt their faith in the midst of prolonged discomfort and powerlessness. Jesus' interaction with Peter came at the end of Jesus reminding the disciples to *feed my sheep*[39] and those who in late-life do so by exercising the gift of *patience* through setting good examples of faithfulness and hope even when they can no longer *do* much of anything. They trust in the Christian faith that they are accepted by God in spite of their best as well as their worst. They accept themselves as human beings created by God and having in some way, however small, joined God in bringing His will to come to pass. They join their Lord in His Gethsemane

---

38. John 21:1819.
39. John 21:17b.

prayer, *"Father, if you are willing, remove this cup from e, yet not m;y will but thine be done."*⁴⁰

And they follow Jesus in patient waiting by not letting their *". . . hearts be troubled. Believe in God, believe also in me. In my Father's house there are many dwelling places. If it were not so, would I have told you that go to prepare a place for you. . .so that where I am, there you may be also."*⁴¹

This is the Christian hope. It is the essence of spiritual patience and Rolls-Royce Spirituality.

On his death bed at 85+ years, John Wesley was asked if he was still assured of the love of God. He could no longer speak, so the questioner said, "If you still believe, raise your hands" and Wesley's arms went up from his sides and he died with his arms held high—a sure example of the spiritual gift of patience and Rolls-Royce Spirituality.

---

40. Luke 22:42.
41. John 14:13.

7

KINDNESS
The Samaritan Fruit

WE TURN NEXT TO the Spiritual Fruit called *Kindness*. I have labeled it the "Samaritan" fruit after Jesus' parable of the Good Samaritan. The parable could have been named the *kind* Samaritan because *goodness* and *kindness* are practically synonyms. Or are they? Maybe a person could be good, but not kind. But I doubt the reverse would be true. A kind person would almost certainly be a good person.

Perhaps, however Jesus' parable of the Last Judgment (Matthew 25–31ff) would be a better illustration of kindness than the parable of the Good Samaritan. Here Jesus enumerates "kind" activities that are more everyday than those that provoke travelers to stop and help others on the highway. *"I was hungry and you gave me food, I was thirst and you gave me something to drink, I was a stranger and you welcomed me, I was naked and gave me clothing,*

I was sick and you took care of me, I was in prison and you visited me I."[42]

Few of us have had occasion to stop and bind up wounded travelers who have been in automobile accidents or been robbed, as a modern Good Samaritan might do.[43] But I would wager that most Christians would feel judged by Jesus for not having always acted helpfully (i.e., kindly) to neighbors or friends when we see they might need some help, much less when we saw a need in "one of the least of these," to use Jesus' depiction of those others who are less fortunate than we are.

KINDNESS TO THE 'LEAST OF THESE'

In fact, the more I have thought about it, the more convinced I have become of St. Paul's wisdom in including *kindness* in his list of spiritual fruit. Jesus examples are but a few of the practical ways that could show forth our true transcendence of mundane faith. In fact, everyday *kindness* may turn out to be one of the central ways that *identity love* is expressed in Rolls-Royce Spirituality. Interestingly, the scripture combines *love* and *kindness* in the beautiful word *lovingkindness* (e.g., Psalm 25:6 and Isaiah 63:7 where the word is always ascribed to God). So, this means that we are following God's lovingkindness of us when we express the spiritual fruit of love by being kind to others. God's love of us never changes and He treats us kindly when we turn to him for help. Further, the word could be reversed (e.g,. *kindlylove*) in the sense that that God treats us kindly because of his everlasting love of us. We are precious in His sight and we are to treat others as He treats us.

I know of one church that has *In and Out Sundays* about twice a year. On these Sundays, the congregation assembles for a brief worship service and then disperses to a variety of places where

---

42. Matt 25:35 36.

43. In fact, in many places there is a "Good Samaritan Law" that protects people (especially medically trained persons) who stop to help in an accident from litigation that they might incur from those dissatisfied with the help they were given. .

they work about two hours helping in situations or with persons who are in need—i.e., being kind. For several weeks ahead, the Sunday worship bulletin includes a list of options in which members can get involved. These include for example:

- singing hymns in a nursing home
- cleaning up trash left in a nearby park
- listening to homeless people share their stories
- packing and sorting food in a free food pantry
- making up birthing kits for new mothers
- helping clean-up city parks
- sharing with paroled prisoners who are trying to adjust to life
- stuffing back-packs with food for children to take home on weekends
- assisting in the building of a new women's section in a local mission
- visiting with alone (lonely?) people at the bus station.-

Each of these was a kindness event in which church members could participate. Those who did were doing the kind of tasks that Jesus mentioned in Matthew 25.

There may be some "Yes, but . . ." reactions that you might have to such a church program as In and Out Sunday. First, you might say, "Those activities were all contrived. Most of the church members had not thought of doing them before." This is true. But maybe this is the kind of stimulation many people need to be kind. Who is to say that helping at the county food bank on In and Out Sunday did not prompt some church member to go back during the week and become regular workers?

A second "Yes, but .." reaction might be to say, "Those contrived kindness events might give church members a reason *not* to be kind in the opportunities they have every day, such as to give some money to those people who stand at stop-lights and beg." This, too, could be true. I know I often get a guilty feeling when I am waiting for a stop-light to change and there are persons standing ten feet away holding a sign saying they need money for food. I often don't even look at them. And, it is very common to hear people say they don't give to street-corner beggars because they might be using the money to buy drugs or beer. I even heard a preacher report he gave twenty-dollars to a person holding a sign that said she needed that amount of money to catch the bus to take a sick baby home. He was taken aback to see the same woman with the same sign there the next day.

One wonders whether Jesus would use any of these excuses for our not being kind in our day-to-day lives. He does not seem in his parable to have any of these considerations in encouraging his followers to be kind. I should take that back. Jesus made one qualification:

> (the righteous will answer) . . ."Lord, when was it that we saw you hungry and gave you food, or thirsty and gave you something to drink? And when was it that we saw you a stranger and welcomed you, or naked and gave you clothing? And when was it that you sick or in prison and visited you? And the king will answer them, "Truly I tell you, just as you did it to one of the least of these who are members of my family, you did it to me."[44]

I'm guessing Jesus would applaud a church's effort to stimulate kindness in such contrived ways as In and Out Sunday but He (Jesus) would be appalled if those activities were used by some people as an excuse for not being kind to the less fortunate in their everyday lives.

KINDNESS UNDER DURESS

There is another dimension of "kindness" that has not been considered at all in the discussion thus far. This is the kind of kindness that Christians are called to exhibit under duress. Although Jesus did not use the word *kindness* in His teaching in the Sermon on

---

44. Matt 25:37-40.

the Mount (Matthew 5–7), kindness was exactly what he meant when he stated:

> You have heard that it was said, 'An eye for an eye and a tooth for a tooth.' But I say to you, Do not resist and evildoer. But if anyone strikes you on the right cheek, turn the other also; and if anyone wants to sue you and take you to court give your cloak as well; and if anyone forces you to go one mile, go also the second mile. Give to everyone who begs from you, and do not refuse anyone who wants to borrow from you.[45]

Yikes! This puts kindness into a different dimension, does it not? Heretofore, we have been discussing the kind of kindness that we exude out of our abundance, our strength, our comfort, our self-confidence, or our good fortune. Now, we Christians who aspire to Rolls-Royce Spirituality are being called to show kindness when we have been offended, cheated, knocked down, hurt, burglarized, swindled, persecuted, or deceived. This is a tall order.

A Christian friend of mine's experience of being overcharged by an auto-repairman is a concrete example of this type of kindness. He was billed for over $1500 for his car's 60,000 mile checkup. This was a hefty amount but he was assured that the car was thoroughly inspected to prevent future repairs. Two days after he got the car back, a signal came up on the dial indicating that the air conditioner needed repair. When the car was taken back, the repair man stated that the 60,000 check up did not include examining the air conditioner—a justification my friend saw as a ruse for poor workmanship. When he went back to get the car after the air conditioner was repaired, he was presented with an additional $750 bill. My friend felt cheated and deceived.

How should Christians aspiring to Rolls-Royce Spirituality act? Should they intend to show forth the spiritual fruit of kindness in such a situation as this? Jesus' answer to this question is very clear:

---

45. Matt 5:38-42.

> *You have heard that it was said 'You shall love your neighbor and hate your enemy.' But I say to you, Love your enemies and pray for those who persecute you, so that you may be children of your Father in heaven. . .For if you love those who love you what reward to you have? Do not even the tax collectors do the same? And if you greet only your brothers and sisters, what more are you doing than others? Do not even the Gentiles do the same? Be perfect, therefore, as your heavenly Father is perfect.*[46]

Jesus would take the repair man to lunch.

Another example of being kind under duress is when one gets sick. We have all known people, including Christians, who become terrorists when they are sick. Remaining kind under these conditions is a challenge. Nurses don't come quickly enough, doctors don't explain enough, visitors don't visit often enough! The complaints pile up. Stress can turn into distress. Such personal situations are a true test of self-control—one of Paul's basic spiritual fruits.

Ian Barclay, in his helpful book *Living and Enjoying the Fruit of the Spirit,* tells the story of Robert Louis Stevenson's sojourn in Samoa where he became very ill. But, he

> " . . . continued to show great kindness to the islanders. His condition worsened and he was confined to sitting on the porch of his hut, from which he could only see the dark trees of the jungle. One day he was surprised to see the forest suddenly filled with half-naked savages cutting the trees down. They had heard that Stevenson wanted to see the breakers rolling onto the beach, and because they were so grateful for the many kindnesses he had shown them, they had come to cut a clearway from his hut to the beach. Stevenson wanted to pay them, but they refused, asking only that they might be allowing the name the pathway through the trees. They called it The Road of a Loving Heart."[47]

---

46. Matt 5:4348.
47. Barclay, *Living and Enjoying the fruit.,* 57.

Rolls-Royce Spirituality

This is yet another type of situation where kindness under duress is difficult. This is having a job that involves danger and the use of force. For example, how can a prison guard be kind? The job itself involves dealing with persons that are incarcerated because they have threatened the lives of other people. They often rebel against prison rules or plot against those who control them. Guards must always be on-guard for their own safety. Can they be kind and still do their job well? It can be done but requires strong self-control. I once heard a group of parolees share about their experiences in prison. Only one of them spoke of a guard who was nice, much less kind. But even in these types of circumstances it is possible to be kind.

Such kindness in the midst of duress may make *kindness* the toughest fruit in all of St. Paul's list. However, *kindness* in good times and bad will remain a significant component of the lifestyle of those who aspire to Rolls-Royce Spirituality. Transcending mundane faith in a way this feels very irrational to those who think kindness has its limits. Even good Christians might feel that if they do not defend themselves they will lose their self-respect. They might even remind us that Jesus said that the rich young ruler should love his neighbor *As Himself*. They might claim that if they followed Jesus' teaching to be kind to those who offend us is a surefire way to become depressed. Yet those who aspire to Rolls-Royce Spirituality know that no life experience that can be imagined is powerful enough to take away God's love—the ultimate source of all our self-confidence. Paul's words should be a constant reminder of this foundation for the fruit of kindness:

> *"Who (or what) will separate us from the love of Christ? Will hardship, or distress, or persecution, or famine, or nakedness, or peril, or sword?.No, in all these things, we are more than conquerors, through him who loved us For I am convinced that neither death, nor life, nor angels. Nor rulers, nor things present, nor things to come, nor powers, nor height, nor depth, nor anything else in all creation will be able to separate us from the love of God in Christ Jesus our Lord."*[48]

48. Rom 8:35 39.

8

GENEROSITY
The Stewardship Fruit

I HAVE LABELED *GENEROSITY* the *Stewardship Fruit* because I think that the theological foundation for Paul including generosity in his list of spiritual fruit lies in the essential conviction that God is the owner of everything, both natural and created. We human beings are but the *Stewards*, not the *Owners* of those possessions for the brief duration of our life-times. The first two verses of Psalm 24 state this without equivocation:

"The earth is the Lord's and all that is in it, the world, and those who live in it;

for he has founded it on the seas, and established it on the rivers."[49]

As a child, I learned these verses in the King James idiom—and still prefer it when it states the majestic proclamation: *The earth is the Lord's and* THE FULNESS THEREOF *and* ALL THAT DWELL THEREIN. "Fulness" implies everything and everybody.

---

49. Psalm 24.

Rolls-Royce Spirituality

"All that dwell therein" is an explanation of "fulness" and implies every creature that moves plus every inanimate thing that exists—both natural and human. If it exists or is created (or dwells) it belongs to God. The gist of both translations is the same: though we might live under another fantasy, we and nothing we possess, belongs to us; we are simply *Stewards* (i.e., caretakers, attendants, custodians, representatives).

This same point could be made about the "sale" of Manhattan by the Indians for $24. Mark Kulansky, the author of the interesting book *The Big Oyster*, on the development of the oyster trade in the United States, wrote: "...in Lenape culture, and in most North American culture, the concept of owning land did not exist...Land was created by God and could not be owned any more than someone could buy a piece of the ocean, lay claim to the sky, or purchase a star."[50]

STEWARDSHIP RESULTS IN GENEROSITY

Generosity is an essential characteristic of "stewardship." It can apply to the giving of time and effort as well as to the donating of money and goods. Although not always consciously related to Biblical teaching, it is amazing how quickly citizens responded generously to the devastating tornado in Oklahoma and the hurricanes in New Orleans and New England. They quickly sent money to the Red Cross and/or traveled to the disasters to physically help in the clean-up.

While public generosity is astonishing and commendable, the reported statement of the philosopher Cicero is worth repeating. He reportedly said, "Society and the human fellowship will be best served if we confer the most kindness on those with whom we are most closely associated." Cicero's comment is pertinent in light of our major concern, namely, "how to exercise generosity within Rolls-Royce Spirituality in our behavior with those we meet

---

50. Kulansky, *The Big Oyster*, 39.

in daily relationships." Here we can look to the teachings/parables of Jesus and the example of the first-century Christian church.

Luke 11:37–41 (NRSV) tells of Jesus at dinner with a Pharisee who complained that Jesus did not wash up before the meal: *"Now you Pharisees clean the outside of the cup and of the dish, but inside you are full of greed and wickedness. You fools! Did not the one who made the outside make the inside also? So give for alms those things that are within; and see, everything will be clean for you."*[51]

Peterson's paraphrase of this Scripture is also worth noting:

> *I know now you Pharisees burnish the surface of your cups and plates so they sparkle in the sun, but I also know your insides are maggoty with greed and secret evil. Stupid Pharisees! Didn't the One who made the outside also make the inside? Turn both your pockets and your hearts inside out and give generously to the poor; then your lives will be clean, not just your dishes and your hands.*[52]

GENEROSITY STEMS FROM THE HEART

In the phrase "turn both your pockets and your hearts inside out" Jesus intuitively speaks to the inner dynamic of generosity i.e., our *hearts*, where the real issue of stewardship spirituality lies. This illustrated the wisdom of St. Paul in including *generosity* among his list of spiritual fruit. Those who are truly generous are acting out of internal stewardship awareness, not simply making a show to impress others. Only God knows what lies beneath generous acts but Jesus wanted to make it clear to the Pharisees what these acts truly meant. It could have been that some Pharisees were, indeed, heart-felt stewards but Jesus was aware of how often this is not true. The label "Pharisee" has come to stand for pretense, hypocrisy, and deceit. As the old saying goes, "Today's Christians often become tomorrow's Pharisees." Only constant self-analysis is

---

51. Luke 11:37–41.
52. Peterson, *The Message*, 16–32.

necessary for this not to happen. Rolls-Royce Spirituality cannot live where Pharisee-ism exists.

GENEROSITY IN THE NEW TESTAMENT CHURCH

This leads to the example of the early Christian church. Acts 2:42 is very clear about the generous nature of their fellowship. They shared all things *in common.*

> ...They devoted themselves to the apostles' teaching and fellowship, to the breaking of bread and the prayers.
>
> Awe came upon everyone, because many wonders and signs were being done by the apostles. All who believed were together and had all things in common; they would sell their possessions and goods and distribute the proceedings to all as any had need. Day by day, as they spent much time together in the temple, they broke bread at home and ate their food with glad and generous hearts.[53]

It is very clear that the earliest Christian fellowship was essentially generous in its practice. They lived communally and combined their wealth. They shared what they had with everyone as there was a need. It is clear that they assumed, as good Jews whose Messiah had come, that they were called to return to the earliest teaching of their faith that they were to live as good stewards of God's creation and that everyone was to be supported equally and generously. They took over the Old Testament teaching of "Sabbath Economics" whereby the practices of sharing equally, working six days, and worshiping and resting on the seventh were assumed to be the will of God for His kingdom on earth—although Sunday, the day of Resurrection supplanted Saturday, the day of Rest for Christians.

---

53. Acts 2:42.

GENEROSITY IN THE EARLY CHURCH

As Ched Myers, the author of the term "Sabbath Economics" notes, radical generosity was assumed by a good Messianic Jew to be foundational for living the new life in Christ.[54] The story of a couple that violated this belief is clearly illustrated in the experience of Ananias and Saphira related in Acts 5:1ff. Here a husband and wife sold a piece of property and withheld back some of the proceeds from the church. The words of Peter to Ananias are haunting but profound:

Peter asked, "Why has Satan filled your heart to lie to the Holy Spirit and to keep back part of the proceeds of the land? While it remained unsold, did it not remain your own? And after it was sold, were not the proceeds at your disposal?

How is it that you have contrived this deed in your heart? You did not lie to us but to

God!" Now when Ananias heard these things, he fell down and died (as did his wife when confronted).[55]

Note how Peter did the same thing as did Jesus; he located the real issue of generosity (and Stewardship) in the Heart. Outer behavior had to be controlled by inner motivation. In the case of Ananias and Saphira, their heart failure led them to presume they could get by with duplicity. But Peter had the insight to confront them and they lost their lives.

This was the first century and this is the twenty-first. What is the difference for those who would aspire to Rolls-Royce Spirituality today? The basic answer is NONE—there is no difference. Chad Myers notes that God's will for creation did fit easily in to creation's pre-history hunter-gatherer time. He contends that God's will had not changed by the time of first century semi-urban and budding capitalistic in which Jesus lived. Further, God's will has remained the same in our thoroughly independent culture of today– as radical at that might seem.

---

54. Myers, *Sabbath Economics*, 3.
55. Acts 5:35.

Rolls-Royce Spirituality

The teachings of Jesus reflect a change from the hunter-gather mentality into a capitalistic, money based, social-class based economy such as the one in which we live in the modern twenty-first century. Jesus was sensitive to this type of setting—as can be seen in such parables as the Laborers in the Vineyard (Matt.20:1ff), the Prodigal Son (Luke:15:11ff) , the Unforgiving Servant (Matt. 19:23ff), the Wicked Tenants (Mark. 12:1ff), the Talents (Luke 19:11–27), the Rich Fool (Luke:12:13 ff), the Dishonest Manager (Luke:16:1 ff). They illustrate a culture similar to today where some accumulate wealth, some get by but where others lose and become debtors, and where the poor barely survive.

RADICAL GENEROSITY—TODAY'S IDEAL

Radical *generosity* is still the ultimate will of God for life today—for us and those we know personally as well as for society at large. Stewardship generosity grounded in the continuing will of God in creation and seen in Jesus as well as sustained by the Holy Spirit is an integral component of Rolls-Royce Spirituality as noted appropriately in Paul's list of fruit of the Spirit.

Being truly generous in the sense that God intends may make *generosity* the most difficult of all the fruit of the Spirit for the modern Christian. I still remember my professor of Christian Ethics who stated without equivocation that Christians should put no money into insurance and should give away all their money every month that they did not need to survive. This clearly resembled what is called a "zero-based economy" where a person gives away all that is left and starts anew with nothing. My professor suggested Christians should follow Jesus' admonition to the Rich Young Ruler ". . .*you lack one thing, go sell what you own, and give the money to the poor, and you will have treasure in heaven; then come follow me.*"[56]

Mark's side comment is very insightful: *When he* (the rich young ruler) *heard this, he was shocked and went away grieving for*

---

56. Mark 10:17ff.

he had many possessions.[57] One wonders how typical this reaction might be to the average Christian today. I cannot imagine how Jesus would change any word in his teaching for the modern believer who probably lives in a society that admires the achievement of success and the amassing of personal wealth.

Our Savior elaborated His advice to followers both then and now in Matthew 6:31–32 (NRSV) by saying, *"Therefore, do not worry, saying, 'What will we eat?' or 'What will we drink?' or 'What will we wear?' For it is the Gentiles who strive for all these things."*[58]

Jesus must have realized such challenges were pretty rare in his day because in this same section he depicted his followers as "you of little faith."[59]

I simply do not know any Christian who meets this standard. For those aspiring to Rolls-Royce Spirituality, radical generosity should, however, remain as an aspiration. It is a standard that has not changed from Jesus' time to the present.

---

57. Mark 10:22.
58. Matt 6:31–32.
59. Matt 6:30.

9

GENTLENESS
The Tenderizing Fruit

TO BE GENTLE MEANS to be mild, soothing, lenient, amiable, careful, embracing, tender. The opposite of gentleness is roughness. Roughness means to be violent, harsh, stern, demanding, impatient, angry, cross, loud, defensive, cruel, blunt. I have been both gentle and rough in my dealing with others. I suspect you have, too. I do not have to think very long about examples—particularly when I think of driving my car, that role where I seem most vulnerable.

I used to live about three blocks from a Nissan dealership where I would take my 1984 pickup truck for service from time to time. Early one morning after I had a hearty breakfast and was rested after a good night sleep, I got in the truck and drove slowly to the dealership. Just as I attempted to turn into the service line, a car coming from the opposite direction slowed down then sped up. The driver seemed a bit unsure of himself. I guessed this was his first time there. He turned quickly in front of me, causing me to brake quickly to avoid hitting him. I smiled and waved him on. He smiled and mouthed, 'Thank you.' I was being gentle.

However, the driver of the car behind me saw what I had done. He was in a hurry. I could see his scowl of disapproval that I had let a car to get in front of us. He pulled out from behind me and swerved around in front of me. This frustrated me and I got angry. I sped up and would not let him in. I became defiant. I blew my horn. I forced him to take his place in line and said to myself, "That bully, I won't let him break in line ahead of me." I switched from gentleness to roughness all within a five minute period.

While I didn't do it this time, on another occasion I might have sworn at him and even gestured in a vulgar way had he succeeded in bullying his way in front of me. Some time ago, I heard about a chart of the use of fingers in traffic. It is humorous, but probably accurate, description, for many of us who get frustrated in traffic from time to time. I picture it below. Do you agree?

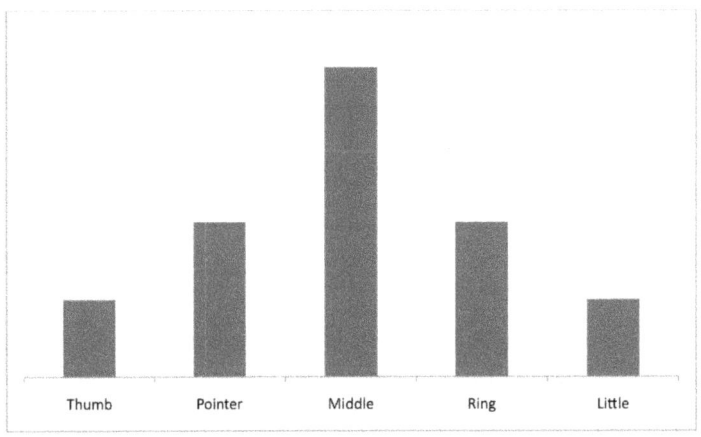

Most of us can identify with this bar graph. It graphically portrays how easy it is to be rough, instead of gentle, in driving. We are all familiar with the term "road rage" that labels those situations where errors in driving or differences of opinion about who caused accidents provoke immense anger among drivers—even among fairly mild-mannered persons. Remaining gentle under stress is a difficult task. St. Paul included *gentleness* in his list of fruit knowing that we needed the Holy Spirit if we would ever be able to remain gentle under all the situations of life.

JESUS ON MEEKNESS, HUMILITY, AND GENTLENESS

Jesus told a parable that illustrated this truth. As he was dining at the home of a Pharisee, Jesus noted that many rushed to claim places of honor. He then said:

> *When you are invited by someone to a wedding banquet, do not sit down at the place of honor, in case someone more distinguished than you has been invited by your host, who invited both of you, may come and say to you, "Give this person your place," and then in disgrace you would start to take the lowest place. But when you are invited, go and sit down at the lowest place, so that when your host comes, he may say to you, 'Friend, move up higher'; then you will be honored in the presence of all who sit at the table with you. For all who exalt themselves will be humbled and those who humble themselves will be exalted.*[60]

Jesus, like Paul, was a keen student of human nature. He knew how easy pride and self-enhancement cause us to barge in to situations and claim our rights. Jesus promises that we will be taken care of in the final analysis if we begin by being self-effacing or gentle instead of rough and demanding. Here, humility could easily be a synonym for gentleness.

Sounds a bit manipulative, doesn't it? It seems like being humble is a sure way to be recognized and honored eventually. It looks like taking the lowest seat is a guarantee that one will be seated closer to the front of the banquet. Even in the third Beatitude, Jesus appeared to promise such a bargain when he states,

---

60. Luke 14:8–11.

GENTLENESS

"Blessed are the meek for they shall inherit the earth."[61] (Matthew 5:5, NRSV)

However, there is one glaring fact is often overlooked in both the parable of seating at the banquet and the third Beatitude. In both cases, the outcome is 'given' rather than being 'earned' or guaranteed. Being given a place of honor at the banquet is something that hosts do on their own initiative and passing down and inheritance is something decided upon by the one who owns the earth—God. In neither case does being meek and gentle guarantee the outcome. The outcome is a gift, not an hourly wage. And this is the reason that *gentleness* is included in Paul's list of spiritual fruit. Being gentle is a result of something done for persons by Almighty God in Christ Jesus our Lord when the Holy Spirit penetrates the hearts of believers so that they cease being arrogant and start being humble. This is the miracle of the gospel. And this sort of miracle is immediate, spontaneous, and certain as can be seen in the confession of one of the thieves who was crucified alongside Jesus. He confessed his faith by saying, "Jesus, remember me when you come into your kingdom," an admission of faith to which Jesus responded "Truly, I tell, today you will be with me in Paradise."[62]

In his book on Spain, *Iberia*, James Michener told of an incident in which he showed gentleness in waiting in line to buy a ticket to a bull fight. He was fourth in line as he waited for the ticket window to open but others shoved in front of him until he was fourteenth when the first ticket was sold. By one o'clock, after the ticket window had been open for five hours, he was twelfth. Michener laughed and said to a salesman from Texas, "Let's just see if they will let people push ahead of us and make us wait all day before selling us a ticket. "A policeman who was standing nearby saw what happened, "They want all you tourists to buy tickets from scalpers on the street." They finally sold the two men tickets in the morning of the second day.

---

61. Matt 5:5.
62. Luke 23:42.

Michener remained calm and laughed about the incident.[63] Can you image not getting mad if you had been treated that way when all you wanted to do was to buy a ticket? Most of us would have become livid. We would have become arrogant and insisted better treatment. How was Michener able to withstand the pressure and remain calm in this situation?

One possible answer was he was not under any time pressure; he decided to make a joke of the situation and he had the strength of a companion who agreed to share the pressure with him. Thinking of a parallel, Christians may often be rushed and may not think the situation is a joke, but do have a companion, the Holy Spirit, who can stand with them in the midst of the stress and strain of life. Remembering that this Holy Spirit is the spirit of the God who created them and Jesus Christ who redeemed them, Christians can answer St. Paul's question, *"Will hardship, or distress, or persecution, or famine, or nakedness, or peril, or the sword* (separate us from the love of Christ)?"[64] with the proclamation, *"No, in all these things we are more than conquerors through him who loved us."*[65]

REACTING WITHOUT RETALIATION

There was a humorous story that circulated some time ago of an airline agent on who pressure was put by a demanding traveler. It happened when there was a long line of persons waiting to check their bags and obtain an assigned seat. A man back in the line became frustrated at how long the process was taking so he stormed to the front of the line and railed at the agent for being so slow. He wanted the agent to take his bags immediately. The agent calmly explained she was doing her best and would get to him as soon as she could. Some moments later when he got to the front of the line, he was still very angry and threatened to have her fired. She remained calm and served him as fast as she could. She did not

---

63. Michener, *Iberia*, 265.
64. Rom 8:35b.
65. Rom 8:37.

GENTLENESS

get flustered or return his anger. The next person in line said to the agent, "How do you stand such rudeness? I noted that you remained calm when he lost his temper." "Well," the agent replied, "He is traveling to Dallas, but his bags are going to Los Angeles."

One of the unique incidents where *being gentle* is recorded in the Old Testament accounts of the death of Absalom, David's son. David defended himself against Absalom who was trying to overthrow Him and become king himself. This type of mutiny was not uncommon. However, having a son attempt to kill his father was almost unknown. Fighting broke out between the armies loyal to David as well as to Absalom.

David was deeply disturbed to be at war with his son. As his soldiers left for the battle front, he gave this order to his generals *"Deal gently for my sake with the young man Absalom. And all the people heard when the king gave orders to all the commanders concerning Absalom."*[66]

This story has a very poignant, sad but understandable ending. As the battle raged, Absalom, who had very long hair, was left hanging from the branch of a tree as his hair got caught and his mule rode away. When this was reported to Joab, one of David's generals, he asked the soldier why he did not kill Absalom, who was hanging helplessly from the branch of the tree. The soldier replied that he did not kill him because it would be reported to David who had given the order to be gentle with his son. Joab, who had been given the direct order, ran his spear through Absalom and killed him.

As news that his army was winning the battle was brought to David, he inquired about his son. "Is it well with the young man Absalom?" When told of Absalom's death, "The king was deeply moved and went to the chamber over the gate, and wept; and he went, he said, 'O my son, Absalom, my son, my son! Would I had died instead of you, O Absalom, my son, my son!'"[67]

A more vivid example of being gentle under distress would be hard to find. David ordered them to be gentle with his arch

---
66. 2 Sam 18:5.
67. 2 Sam 18:33.

enemy—his son. And when he learned that he had won the battle but that his son, Absalom, had been killed, he wept bitterly and stated that he wished he had died in Absalom's place. Absolutely amazing!

One of my granddaughters recently moved to Portland, Oregon. She is a young woman in her mid-twenties. While her new job requires her to be on her feet much of the day, she decided to join a Roller Derby group for fun and exercise. This was a surprise to me and my wife. Growing up she was a mild, slightly timid, fairly quiet person, so we would never had predicted she would participate in such a raucous, active sport as Roller Derby. She explained that she had been required to not only purchase sturdy skates but a whole host of protective gear designed to soften the rough confrontations with other skaters. Because she is fairly new to the sport, she has a red ribbon attached to her helmet. This is a signal to other more experienced skaters to not bump into her from the side or back until she improves. As she becomes more skilled the color of the ribbon will change, but until then she is treated gently.

GENTLENESS GROUNDED IN IDENTITY LOVE

The lesson of my Roller Derby granddaughter's experience is not how to protect ourselves in a rough and tumble world but how we who should practice Rolls-Royce Spirituality with all the other skaters in our lives—we should be gentle! We should act as if everyone we meet has a red ribbon attached to their helmets. We are not to bump them from the side or rear. We should be gentle. In fact, as time goes on and we become more spiritual in the game of life, we will probably become poorer, rather than better, players on the Roller Derby team. Ha!

In fact, gentleness is grounded in *identity love*—the awareness that everyone is like ourselves: a unique human creation uniquely endowed with the ability to love and be loved. Thus, we are to avoid any action that would impede their development. The Greek words for gentleness is applied to parents dealing with misbehaving children and Paul catches this flavor in recommending, "...*if anyone is detected in a transgression, you who have received the Spirit should restore such a one in the spirit of gentleness.*"[68]

He is even more explicit in his words to the church at Rome:

> *Welcome with open arms fellow believers who don't see things the way you do. And don't jump all over them every time they do or say something you don't agree with—even when it seems that they are strong on opinions but weak in the faith department. Remember, they have their own history to deal with. Treat them gently.*[69]

Gentleness is a fitting last fruit in the list because it is the very essence in which love should be undertaken. It is like a perfume or essence that should hover over and penetrate joy, peace, patience, kindness—even faithfulness, the fruit we will consider in the final chapter. Jesus and Paul both thought of gentleness as the basic attitude that should surround all else that the Holy Spirit intends for everyday life. It is essential for Rolls-Royce Spirituality.

---

68. 2 Cor 6:1.
69. *The Message*, 14:1.

10

FAITHFULNESS
The Practice Makes Perfect Fruit

I LABELED THIS CHAPTER on *Faithfulness* as the "*Practice Makes Perfect*" *fruit*, because a major dimension of being "faithful" is to act on any new insight, learning, conviction, or skill again and again until it becomes habitual and we do it without thinking. I suspect that most of us know this as we think about New Year's resolutions we made but do not faithfully practice. They fill our "might have been" waste cans.

NEW LEARNING HAS TO BE PRACTICED

I know this truth well when I think of the foreign languages that were required for my doctoral degree. I have not utilized them enough for them to have any meaning for me today. Some time ago I became interested in what was written about religion in the early psychoanalytic journal, *Imago*—all of whose articles were published in German. I tried to do my own translations. I got no further than the first page of the first article. "Practice makes perfect." I once knew German well enough to read and/or translate German into English—but no more. The same will be of the *fruit of the Holy Spirit* if we do not become faithful in practicing them until they become "perfect." If these fruit do not become habits, the day will come when they, like my German, become useless to us.

Because the story of Jesus is so impressive—God among us! God speaking a language we can understand!—there is the danger that we will be impressed, but not empowered. As the spectacular dimensions of the Christ event dawn upon us, we could easily become enthusiastic spectators, and then let it go at that. We could become admirers of Jesus, generous with our oohs and ahs, and in our better moments inspired to imitate Him—but not faithful followers.

OLD HABITS ARE HARD TO BREAK

There is an old anonymous poem that states this truth very well:

> The sermon now ended, each turned and descended;
> The eels went on eeling, The peels went on peeling
> Much delighted were they, but preferred the old way.

'Preferring the old way' is natural from a psychological point of view. Old habits have a strenuous hold on us. This becomes ever truer the older we become. Mundane faith can exert a hold on us that is very, very difficult to break. My family is a good example. We have been regular attendees at Sunday worship service most of our lives. Organs have always accompanied our singing. Recently, our church has included the music of 'praise bands'—replete with guitars and drums plus the clapping of hands. We are very uncomfortable with this and often avoid services where the band plays. If we put Rolls-Royce Spirituality into practice, how would we behave?

These fruit of the Spirit are a *new way* to live. They will always be at war with the *old way* of mundane faith. There is a true saying that we have all heard that goes like this 'use it or lose it.' This saying speaks to the unavoidable need to diligently practice the fruit or we will lose them, just as I lost my ability to translate German into English. This is the reason Paul includes *faithfulness* in his fruits of the Holy Spirit. *Faithfulness* is a crucial component in our efforts to achieve Rolls-Royce Spirituality. The answer to the age-old question of whether old dogs can learn new tricks is unquestionably "Yes" but "new tricks" will become "past fads" if not faithfully practiced.

As I read Eugene Peterson's paraphrase of the Bible, I am often impressed with the way he puts Scripture into words that are both poignant and profound. In expressing Moses blessing of the children of Israel along their way toward the Promised Land, Peterson states the words of Moses in a manner that can easily be applied to the possibility of faithfully putting into practice Paul's fruit of the Holy Spirit. Moses says:

> *This commandment that I'm commanding you today isn't too much for you, it's not out of your reach. It's not on a high mountain—you don't have to get mountaineers to climb the peak to bring it down to your level and explain it before you can live it. And it's not across the ocean—you don't have to send sailors to get it, bring it back, and then explain it before you can live it. The word is right here and now—as near as the tongue in your mouth, as near as the heart in our chest. Just do it!*[70]

JUDGING PROGRESS IN SPIRITUAL DEVELOPMENT

So far we have reflected on the problem of adapting to a new way to be Christian (i.e., Rolls-Royce Spirituality). Performing all of Paul's eight fruit well all day and every day may be quite a task. It's not like a New Year's resolution to walk an hour each day—one thing at one time every day. Paul's Spiritual fruit is a resolution to do many

---

70. Deut 30: 11–14, *The Message*, 295.

things, every day, in all relationships, from morning to evening. Like the little boy I mentioned earlier who got frustrated because he could not love all his little cars at the same time, practicing Rolls-Royce Spirituality may feel overwhelming. What we need is some model that will keep the ideal ever before us and will honor our progress, yet prevent us from becoming depressed and giving up.

This endeavor to practice all the fruits of the Spirit reminded me of a similar need acknowledged by the Ethics Committee of the American Psychological Association (APA) on which I once served. We were the committee that set the ideal standards of care for clinical psychologists who worked with disturbed clients all day long. We stated that the quality of service we provided to them should be very good regardless of whether we counseled them at 8:00 in the morning or at 8:00 in the evening. Our own fatigue at the end of the day should not cause our minds to wander or our own needs to compromise the quality of service we offered. Attention to their needs during the whole hour we were with them should be our goal. When we set this standard, we knew it would be hard to achieve in every situation. It required a number of behaviors that differed from client to client but it held up an ideal that always put the needs of the client above our fatigue or personal preoccupations. Yet it was a supreme value to which every clinical psychologist should aspire.

So it is with love, joy, kindness, generosity, gentleness, peace, patience and self control—the Spiritual fruit of Rolls-Royce Spirituality. Those who want to transcend mundane faith should aspire to express them every day, in every way, with every person. But let us admit, along with the Ethics Committee of the American Psychological Association, these are ideals that are very difficult to achieve.

What we did as an Ethics Committee was to set this standard as an ideal to which every clinical psychologist should aspire, but at the same time set a level at which we would judge that service to be inferior and require the psychologist to appear before us for remediation or loss of the license to practice. Perhaps we should consider something similar to the way we think about Rolls-Royce Spirituality. We could, for example, state that the very highest ideal would be for a Christian who aspired to transcend mundane faith to express all the fruit of the Spirit all day with every person they met. The opposite would also be true. We might say that the very worst thing a Christian who aspired to transcending mundane faith could do would be to express none of the fruit of the Spirit with any of the people they met all day long.

What I suggest is this: keep a "Win Journal." This journal would be a broader adaptation of the procedure I described in the chapter on Love. The process would go like this: contract with another person who is aspiring toward Rolls-Royce Spirituality to share with each other on a regular basis your episodes in which you put into practice one or more of the fruit of the Holy Spirit. Start small. Love should come first. Start first with those you meet at church. Theoretically, this should be the easiest place for your good intentions to work best. Would you not assume that church is the place where other people gather who are trying to be Christian to some extent in their lives. They should be the place where others already love, or at least like, one another. We know this is not always true, so the effort to start with *identity love* may be more difficult than we first thought. Still it is the place to begin.

After the two of you judge that Love is beginning to become a habit, move beyond the church walls. Center your attention on your families. Here you will find the going a little more challenging. Here the difference between "liking" and "loving" may be starker. As the mother I mentioned earlier stated, "I don't like my daughter, but I love her." That is often true in families. In families, the problem of the difference between what we should do may complicate how we feel. Black sheep graze the pastures of most families. But the ideal of *identity love* remains the same.

You can probably anticipate where my method is moving. Rolls-Royce Spirituality requires attention and concentration. One might say, it becomes the central preoccupation for those for those who want to transcend mundane faith. Adding Self Control and the other spiritual fruit one by one to our new habitual way of living is the ultimate goal to which becoming spiritual at a Rolls-Royce level requires.

A THEOLOGICAL COMMENT ON THE TASK

Remaining 'faithful' to the task of attaining Rolls-Royce Spirituality will likely require a persistence beyond anything to which you have ever committed yourself before. St. Paul speaks encouragement to us with the following words: *"I don't know about you, but I'm running hard for the finish line. I'm giving it everything I've got. No sloppy living for me! I'm staying alert and in top condition. I'm not going to get caught napping, telling everyone else all about it and then missing out myself."*[71]

However, all our attempts to express fruit of the spirit in our daily lives still come under the forgiving love of God who challenges and empowers each of us to become Rolls-Royce Christians yet who understands we are human for, as Scripture suggests, "We hold these truths in earthen vessels."[72] We remain human until we die.

Most importantly, we are not in the business of proving ourselves to God. As Ephesians 2:8 (NRSV) points states: *"For by grace you have been saved through faith, and this is not of your own doing; it is the gift of God—not the result of works, so that no one may boast."*[73]

Our aspiration toward Rolls-Royce Spirituality is not an achievement that somehow will impress God or St. Peter at the time of our death. Instead, we should look at ourselves as human beings, who live at this time and in this place and have the precious privilege of playing a faithful role in Holy History. As the Harvard theologian, Gordon Kaufman, suggested, "(God). . .created men (sic) to *work* in his world as "laborers together with God" (1 Cor.3:9, NRSV) as co-creators in the historical process through which he(sic) is creating

---

71. 1 Cor 9:2427. *The Message*, 1795.
72. 2 Cor 47.
73. Eph 2:8.

Rolls-Royce Spirituality

his kingdom."[74] Nevertheless, in a paradoxical manner, we should still aspire to become fully perfect (i.e., attain full Rolls-Royce spirituality and transcend Mundane Faith) by at least "five minutes before we die," as John Wesley reportedly advised.

Such a perfection goal would be Faithfulness incarnate. Below is a picture of Allen Swift, a man who had driven his 1928 Rolls-Royce since his father gave it to him as a present upon his high school graduation. He died in 2005 at 102 years. He had driven the car faithfully for over a million miles. Swift donated both the car and the Verizon building in which it sits in the Transportation Section of the New Springfield History Museum, Springfield, Massachusetts. This Rolls-Royce still runs like a Swiss Watch.

I end where I began—with a personal commitment to become a Christian who aspires toward Roll-Royce Spirituality and I invite you to join me. My good friend Guy Aydelott expressed it well in the second verse of his hymn "Come, All You People"

Come, all you disciples who have open hearts and join the grand parade of those who step the dance of faith,

"Who is our neighbor," asked the Pharisees and God is asking you

---

74. Kaufman, *Systematic Theology*, 297.

Your neighbor is the one in need and love allows a wondrous deed;

God's way we will pursue.

Praise to the one who leads the grand parade; who leads us day by day!

And, as we walk and as we dance, we shout "Hosanna" as we advance to the

> Truth, the Life, and the Way.[75]

". . . but those that wait on the Lord shall renew their strength, they shall mount up with wings like eagles, they shall run and not be weary. They shall walk and not faint."[76]

---

75. *Come, All You People,* unpublished hymn by Guy E. Aydelott—reprinted by permission.

76. Isa 40:31.

Bibliography

Barklay, Ian Newton. *Living and enjoying the fruit of the Spirit.* Chicago, IL: Moody Press, 1975.
Erikson, Erik H. *Identity and the Life Cycle.* Chicago, IL: W.W. Norton & Company, 1959.
Freud, Sigmund. *The Future of an Illusion (Translate by W.D. Robson-Scott).* Garden City, NY: Doubleday, 1958.
Hale-Evans, Ron. *Mind Performance Hacks: Tips and Tools for Overclocking Your Brain.* Sebastopol, CA: O'Reilly Media, Inc., 2006.
Hillenbrand, Laura. *Unbroken: A World War II Story of Survival, Resilience, and Redemption.* New York: Random House, 2010.
Kaufman, Gordon D. *Systematic Theology: A Historical Perspective.* New York: Charles Scribner's Sons, 1968.
Kurlansky, Mark. *The Big Oyster: History on the Half Shell.* New York: Random House, 2006.
Malony, H. Newton. *When Getting Along Seems Impossible: Straightforward Help to Reduce Conflict and Stress at Home, at Work, and at Church.* Old Tappan, NJ: Revell, 1989.
Mayer, John D., and Peter Salovey. "Emotional intelligence and the construction and regulation of feelings." *Applied & Preventive Psychology, Vol 4(3),* 1995: 197–208.
Myers, Ched. *The Biblical Vision of Sabbath Economics.* Washington D.C.: Tell the Word, Church of the Saviour, 2001.
Peterson, Eugene H. *The Message: The Bible in Contemporary Language.* Colorado Springs, CO: NavPress Publishing Group, 2005.
Pfister, Oskar. "The Illusion of the Future (Die Illusion einer Zunkunft)." *Imago,* 1928: 149–184.
Remen, M.D., Rachel Naomi. *My Grandfather's Blessing: Stories of Strength, Refuge, and Belonging.* New York: The Berkley Publishing Group, 2000.
Shakespeare, William, and edited by Ralph M. Sargent. *As You Like It.* Baltimore: Penguin Books, 1970.
The Holy Bible containing the Old and New Testaments (New Revised Standard Version). National Council of the Churches of Christ, 1989.

The United Methodist Book of Worship. Nashville, TN: The United Methodist Publishing House, 1992.

Thibault, Jane Marie, and Richard L. Morgan. *Pilgrimage into the Last Third of Life*. Nashville, TN: Upper Room Books, 2012.

Tillich, Paul. *The Courage to Be*. New Haven, CT: Yale University Press, 1951.

———. *The Shaking of the Foundations*. New York: Charles Scribner Sons, 1948.

Watts, Isaac. "Joy to the World." In *The United Methodist Hymnal*, 246. Nashville, TN: The United Methodist Publishing House, 1989.

www.ingramcontent.com/pod-product-compliance
Lightning Source LLC
Chambersburg PA
CBHW071153090426
42736CB00012B/2320